POWER

OVER

ANXIETY

Hacks to upgrade your health,
feel amazing and conquer your anxiety.

A how to and a self help.
Your journey to a fitter and healthier you.
Break free of anxiety with renewed optimism
and be the person everyone else looks up to.

Christopher Moss

Disclaimer

Power over Anxiety is to guide you on your journey from anxiety to a feeling you can take on the world. I mean it to help you develop yourself into the person I know you can be.

This book deals with a lot of hard topics, but it is inspiring. It is not intended to replace professional help.

I designed this book to be informative and educational. It does not replace medical judgements, therapy or other higher treatments.

I am unable to respond to specific questions or comments about your personal situation, diagnosis, or treatment. I am also unable to give any clinical opinions. If you are in urgent need of assistance, I advise you to contact your local emergency services or local mental health crisis hotlines.

My resources mentioned in this book are used to help and guide you. It is for education and information only. I am not a medical professional. Please do not replace my information for a specialised training and professional judgement of a health care or mental health care professional.

Neither the author nor publisher can be held responsible for the use of the information detailed in this book.

Want a Free Copy of My First Book
HOPE OVER ANXIETY*?*

Please visit:

https://mailchi.mp/f3b44101979d/freeanxietybook

Table of Contents

About the Author

Christopher Moss is a best-selling author in three countries. His first book, *Hope over Anxiety*, was downloaded more than 1,600 times. He is married with two children and lives in Northamptonshire, England. Chris has worked in retail for over 28 years and is currently a store manager, author, and life coach.

Chris has a passion for writing, building life skills, and inspiring others to take control of their anxiety. His mission is to give people who are suffering the skills and tools they can use to break free on their own. To create a life that they want. To utilise the skills they have from anxiety. To be the best version of themselves they can be.

My Story

If you have read *Hope over Anxiety* and *Freedom over Anxiety*, then I would skip this introduction into me. If not, I want to explain to you how I got here.

My story starts when I was just ten years old. Before that I was a quiet, shy and caring boy. Happy to be alone but loved spending time with my two younger brothers. That is until 1st March 1985 when my life changed forever.

My brother died of cancer, aged just twenty months old. He had his eye removed before this but we thought it was gone. How wrong we were. I remember him laying on the settee unable to do anything. Just laying there. My fun-loving, full-of-beans brother. Lifeless, a shadow of himself. He stopped eating. He stopped playing. Something was wrong. I knew that.

I remember touching him after his death at the funeral parlour he was cold and grey looking. The shock of how ice cold he was shot up my arm, and I couldn't touch him again.

I watched my family fall apart, and it was all my fault. I got home early one day from school to see my mum grabbing my brother's precious green baby grow close to her chest crying, whaling, pain and suffering pouring out of her. Her cry I can still hear to this day.

My family fell apart, and I blamed myself for all this mess. If it wasn't for me, bringing the chicken pox into the house my brother would still be alive. His body was fighting the cancer it had no other fight to stop this virus. He was in intensive care for a week after the ambulance picked him up from our home. He got more frail, weight fell off him. I was barely recognisable to the boy I saw go just a week earlier.

I still remember the moment they told me he had passed. My dad picked me up from the bus stop after I came home from school. I looked at him; they said no words. I realized, 'He has gone hasn't he?'

I changed after his death. I became even more internalized. The spark had gone. My life was colder, darker a more frightening place. This is when my anxiety arrived. Telling me I am not good enough, telling me I deserve all the pain and suffering I get. Because I killed my brother.

It was my fault when I was sexually abused, it was my fault when I was bullied at school and later at work. It was my fault when I got beaten up at work by a jealous boyfriend.

It was my fault when I got mugged, beaten up badly and thrown head first with my hands behind my back into a tree. Everything was my fault.

Fast Forward to 12th December 2014 5.55am

My life before this ordeal was in tatters. I felt I was consistently failing in my job, with my wife and my children. I used my phone as a blanket to shield me from the world. I hated myself. I was completely lost. We were struggling financially, and I was at constant odds with my wife.

The air was quiet, there was a chill in the air as I walked to work that fateful morning. It was a quick two-minute walk from my home. But I couldn't put my finger on it but something felt wrong. My intuition screamed at me to go back home. I saw no choice who would open the store?

I opened the store; I looked round but saw no one. I entered the building that's when he pounced. Armed with what I thought was a hammer threatening to smash my skull in if I didn't open the safe and give me the contents. The ordeal felt like years. I became almost serine in approach as it became a battle of wills; him demanding I open the safe when there was a twenty-minute timer explaining that I had no control over it. It opens when it is time. Several times he demanded I open it. Each time it would reset. Each time he would lift the hammer to smash my skull in. The third time was an ultimatum; open that safe or die. He was losing his rag. He was getting aggressive.

My battle was with myself. I told myself he was an irate customer. Deal with him, let him have what he wanted and then deal with your own emotions. YOU have control of this. You won't get yourself killed. Your wife deserves a husband, your children deserve their father. Looking back after the ordeal on CCTV I have my hands almost in prayer when talking to the robber.

We got the door open to the safe. Third time VERY lucky. He grabbed the £3,500 and ran off out the back. ALL my life was worth. Such a pitiful sum of money for me.

My Life Defining Moment

Once he had gone, and I organised the store ready for re-open. The police asked me to go home as I was showing signs of shock.

Within days I plummeted into crippling anxiety. My fears of him coming back, he told me he knew where I lived, would play out into my head repeatedly. I would play out the morning again and again. Why didn't I go back home? What would have happened if I opened the store differently, what would have happened if I did this and so on? It was endless.

I lived for the moments I felt nothing. Other times rage, anger and shame would course threw my veins. I would regularly have panic attacks. The thought of leaving the home became one of the biggest challenges I have ever faced. It's a door. It was wide open, there was space. So why oh why couldn't I leave my home? Why would I get a panic attack just thinking about leaving my home? I would battle this every day. I had to take the kids to school, who else would take them. I had to take my dog for a walk. I had to send off my sick note. All of those experiences were huge, painful battles.

I thought of ways I could kill myself without my family seeing me. I thought about slitting my wrists, or perhaps hanging myself, or maybe just ploughing my car into a tree. No one else would get hurt. Only me.

I felt so much shame for the man I had become. I hid my pain from everyone. I wanted to protect them from what I had become. Not seeing me as I was almost didn't make it real.

A big fear of mine was no money. Of letting my family down. I knew I couldn't work in that shop again. I felt unsupported by the company I was working with. But I knew time was running out, and I needed to get back to work. But not there no longer! I got an interview! I travelled to two stores miles away from each other. On the same day. I was determined to succeed. My children and wife depended on me getting another job. I had failed at that one I needed a chance to make up for things. To put my life back. I faked being okay. I faked that everything was okay. I was fine.

I got the job! It took weeks before I got confirmation. But when I did, what a relief. My last paycheck from my previous employer was a big, fat nothing. No money. No support. Left to it. No note, no phone call, no care. I didn't fight it as I felt shame that it was my fault they didn't want to speak. That they didn't care.

Getting back to work took time. I continued to fake being okay. The hunger, that will to survive had become a huge driving force in my life. It wasn't pretty, but it worked. I had taken on death and been given a second chance. I had completely screwed up the first time. But not this one. I have all the experience of the past but now the drive of the future. I will do significantly better than this!

Over the next year I read, listened to YouTube and gained any information on anxiety, how to inspire myself and learn who I am.

I went on a journey of discovery. I learned to like myself; I made my anxiety from a scream to a whimper and I am started writing a book. I had found my calling! My purpose.

For so long I had suppressed the real me for fear of ridicule and being laughed at. I used to show my feelings I used show I cared to people. I used to get called gay and weird. Because I didn't conform to what a boy or man should be.

Not any more! Through my armed robbery ordeal I have taken on my anxiety and won. Spoken to thousands of people about anxiety and helped them. I have become a best-selling author in three countries and I am on my third book.

I have jumped exponentially in the last three years. What I used to tolerate, I no longer. I have found some amazing people on my journey and I have learned who I am. I am thankful for my life coach who has been a huge part of why I have grown so much.

I am so thankful for that life lesson I had. I am better, stronger and happier for the experience.

I read in a book that everyone is a teacher. I like to think it has taught me a few hard truths. I am lucky. And I want to show the world what is possible in life!

The Beginning of Your Journey

Hello, thank you for buying my book Anxiety:Biohacked! I designed this book to help you find an alternative to medication and/or to be in a position you have never hoped to be in!

Supercharge your energy levels and your mind. To feel empowered and energised. To feel the best you have ever felt!

My Dream

I want to help 500,000 people with their anxiety. I want to show that average Joe me can do it, so can you. I have over thirty years of experience struggling with anxiety. My pain will help others.

This is my third book. You can use it as a standalone or alongside the previous two books I've done. If you are following this book, this is the third part of my journey towards breaking anxiety.

I will give you a fresh approach to your anxiety and a great chance of breaking free by focusing on your health whether that is your diet, great mind hacks or supplements.

I will go through all the chapters showing you how you can improve yourself. Then it will be beautifully wrapped up in a seven-day plan. Allowing you to structure it the best way for you.

I am also really excited to reveal some awesome stuff during our journey together in this book. Some things I have recently learned and a few things that have been a huge difference in my life. I feel I have halved my anxiety again since the last book. So I am very excited to give you more tools on the journey. Some of this is repeated but I have kept this book fresh with loads of new content.

This book isn't for everyone. It is for those that:

- Need to make a difference.

- Need to break free of anxiety.

- Need to be in a better state of mind and body. You want to find healthier, better ways, of looking after yourself and giving every chance of being anxiety free.

- Want to find alternatives to antidepressants.

If any of this does not resonate with you, then I would suggest you find another book to read. This is your opportunity to take hold of your life. If you don't feel that's what you want, that's cool. Best now not to read it.

If this is what you want, it's what you need, then awesome. Your new life is just beginning!

I will continue to grow myself. To get my body and my mind to the best it can be. That uses all my skills and tools. To use all the information I've learnt over the last few years.

The putting it all together in one enormous, awesome cocktail. I want to be anxiety free and I want to be the best version of myself that I can be not just for myself for my family. I want the energy levels I had when I was in my twenties. I will, and so can you.

From studies I have read, people I have spoken to and my own experience, taking antidepressants doesn't work. Some individual cases it helps but the medical community are slowly realising this isn't the way forward. There has to be another way. It seems so easy these days to be put on antidepressants. I worry about those people.

All it does is treat the SYMPTOMS OF anxiety not the cause. That gets pushed to one side. It will be there when you come off them. You also have to increase or change your medication to treat the symptoms. Another one of the side effects is suicidal thoughts! People also become addicted to them.

We will discuss what is biohacking and how that can help you in your fight with anxiety. We will discuss the two main steps that will give you the best chance breaking free of anxiety.

Your Mind and Your Body

We look at sleep and how that can be used. We will go in to a little detail about sleep to give you an understanding of how it works. We will show you the process the mind has for sleep. Most people need eight hours of sleep. Well, actually it's seven and a half hours. What's 30 minutes between friends? You need to ensure that you have similar sleeping levels to help you see how important it is to look after your mind and your body is. For you to see what can be achieved in your day by looking after your night.

To give you the best chance every morning, we will look at your brain and what ways we can hack it. We will find fun ways of hacking your mind and body. For example forest bathing and blissing out to music. We will help you learn what superfoods will help you manage your mood and anxiety. We will show you why I would recommend using a crazy yellow pill. What dramatic impact it can have on you. Reducing your anxiety and showing you how you can have the best night's sleep you have ever experienced.

This book won't have much jargon. But there will be some as I explain to you some science stuff. It will be a simple and easy-to-use book packed full of information help to you. I want to avoid causing overwhelm. I won't be giving you information if it is not essential to breaking your anxiety.

I have also added a friend's journey. What they have experienced and how they are now.

I have also set up at the start a section that will show you where you are at now and where you will be at the end of the book. If you follow the course, you will find a giant leap in your progress. But believe you can do it. To track your progress will be an excellent tool to see. Your work on yourself will see tangible results!

Not only breaking free of anxiety, but being free of anxiety! Nothing will give me greater pleasure if you go through this journey and do it!

But that's a challenge you need to take.

I never intended to write a literary, prizewinning book. I try to write my books like I am talking to you. As if you are sitting out in Starbucks with a coffee being open and honest not trying to sugarcoat anything. Seeing my pains, vulnerability, struggles and success. Seeing my mindset and understanding EXACTLY how I have achieved what I have.

The biggest thing we focus on in this book is energy levels as anxiety sufferers. We use too many sugary foods and caffeine to keep us motivated and to keep us going every day. I will teach you some cool biohacks that will show you other ways of energizing yourself without the crash in your mood that caffeine and sugar give.

I will show you how to activate your mind. We will go into things you wouldn't expect. I will show you how to get the best from your body.

I have learnt loads on this subject and I have implemented them all. From internet searches to my own experiments. To YouTube searches. Listening to some of the greatest experts on the subject.

Anxiety isn't just about the mental struggles, it's about physical toll on the body. In this book you will find you will be physically prepared for the battles ahead.

What you eat, how you feel and what you do has a dramatic impact on your mood.

I've also learnt some amazing supplements that will diminish your anxiety but enhance your life. Cool, eh?

You can have more energy with your children. You can have more energy in your life. You can have less brain fog in the mornings. A better life beckons. Dare you choose it?

Something I'll be clear on, I will discuss how you can utilise your body and your mind and your diet to be in the best position with your anxiety. Please do not feel overwhelmed. All that will be discussed will then be packaged into a 7-day action plan that will help you get the structure you need to put this into practice. Like I always do with my books, I've worked hard to make this book simple, easy and as understandable as possible. That you can grasp what works for you and get it done without anxiety taking control.

My Promise

If you follow this book, you will be in the best physical state you've ever been in. You will find your energy levels will be in the best state since your twenties. The healthiest you've ever felt. You'll have more strength, confidence, calm and hopefully anxiety free. You will sleep the best you've ever had. If you follow this book if you implement everything on the list. How amazing is that?

The important thing you get it done. But it has to suit you.

I want you to have a better life. I want you to feel amazing. I want you to have a life beyond your dreams. No longer needing caffeine and sugar fixes to keep you going.

Dare to Dream?

How would it feel to not have the energy crashes, but instead be energized? How would it feel to feel more confident, happier and calmer? Feel in control of your anxiety and your life? See yourself progress? Knowing how much you have improved? How much easier would it be to take on your anxiety? When you feel on top of the world? That's what I want you to feel! That's what I want for you.

Excited to start?

Then read on . . .

How the Book Is Laid out

Each chapter will have an introduction and a promise of how it will help the reader. I shall also try to inspire you with some words of encouragement. We will see what this chapter is about and if you want to skim to the end of the chapter, I have an 'In a Nutshell' that will give all the important bullet points for that chapter at the end.

Where Are You at Right Now?

Before we start this book, I want you to be honest with yourself. I have ten questions I would like you to rate yourself on. Four simple responses. This is a temperature check to see how you are feeling. I will ask the same questions at the end of the book. So keep those answers somewhere safe.

By following this book you will see your progress. I also mean it to prime you and get you ready for what is coming. We will go through a lot of this through the book. Some obvious, some not so.

Ten Questions

Answer the following ways that best describes how YOU feel.

From the following; Never, sometimes, often, all the time

How often do you feel happy?

How calm do you feel?

How good is your sleep?

How easily do you make decisions?

How often do you feel nervous?

How often do you feel irritable and restless?

How often do you feel tired?

How often do you feel sad?

How often do you feel useless?

How often do you struggle to calm down when something upsets you?

Additional questions – These just need to be recorded.

How many cups of caffeine do you drink a day?

How often a day do you meditate? Or practice getting calm?

Your Beliefs

This is for you to write down and review again after you have implemented this book. Please be as honest as possible. This is to see your core beliefs. Where you are at right now. NO judgements. Only YOU will see this.

You can answer these statements with a true or false. What you feel. Coming from your heart. Be completely honest with yourself.

By getting to know what your core beliefs are it will guide and improve you. By understanding your beliefs it gives you insight and YOU see what stories you tell yourself. I find these types of questions fascinating. I have learned a great deal about what I believe in!

- I feel like a victim. Everything is my fault!

- What is wrong with me?

- I don't deserve the best life possible.

- I can't handle failure.

- I can handle rejection.

- I can't take criticism.

- If I work at it, I can have what I want.

- I am good enough.

- Life is too hard.

What Is Biohacking?

'I want to feel better, I want to be better.
And I know just what I will do to achieve it!'

Hacking Your Own Body!

Sounds cool doesn't it? It's a process of making changes to help you feel your best. Through hacking your body's biology. This may seem a scary term, but it really isn't. It's about using your mind and your body to ensure you have the best focus hacking your anxiety.

There are many ways to biohacking. You can use it in so many ways. However, several of those ways are not relevant here. What we are interested in is using different ways to improve your mental and physical state to take on anxiety.

I have had the privilege through my books to be very fortunate to speak to some amazing people at the forefront of biohacking or nutrigenomics.

I will talk more about it in a later chapter. I will say now this is one of most exciting discoveries! I found not just for an anxiety sufferer but for anyone that wants to improve themselves physically and mentally.

Anyone Can Biohack

One of the great things about biohacking is it's individual to each person. We will discuss loads of ways it can help you, but there is something I want to be clear on. I want you see which works for you and what doesn't if things don't work don't do them. I set it out to allow you the mix and match. Giving you the programme that is tailored to suit you and you alone. Giving you the best chance to smash your anxiety.

You will be in the best position you have ever been in, physically and mentally.

You will only need to make small changes to your lifestyle for this to be achieved.

A question: Is being alive enough for you? If the answer is no, then you have the beginnings of being a biohacker.

There are many types of biohacking. I won't go into great detail, I'll only go through the main ones you need to help you with your anxiety.

1 – Nutrigenomics

What Is Nutrigenomics?

According to Dictionary.com it is 'the scientific study of the interaction of nutrition and genes, especially regarding the prevention or treatment of disease'.

Nutrigenomics is a big part of this book. We will talk a lot about it here and in later chapters.

Our bodies are constantly changing. There are cells that last a day. We are learning so much about our bodies and using this information to enhance our lives by activating part of our body to improve ourselves.

I have a chapter later in the book. Something I'm extremely excited to talk to you about. It is a crazy yellow pill. It's something I'm using myself and I've seen a massive improvement in my energy levels. Nutrigenomics is the study of nutritionally manipulating the activity of the body. I will tell you a lot more about later.

2 – Diet

I know I can hear you groaning. Please don't let that put you off. This isn't about losing weight. This isn't about fasting, although it has been proven that you can seriously improve your health. It is about improving what you eat. Which will help you feel in a far better place. It's about helping you feel more energized by removing, or at least reducing, the need for sugar or high sugar contents. As a bonus, it will reduce your mood swings and feel more consistent. Giving you more power over your anxiety.

Become the gatekeeper to your body. What goes into your mouth? You need to have to control of what it is by being consciously aware. There will be times you will have a chocolate bar or sweets or something sugar based. But this needs to be a reward, not something you use regularly.

Write a Food Journal

If you see what you are eating, you will control what happens next. You will see patterns when you eat. You'll understand the emotional side of eating.

How Can We Use Biohacking for Our Anxiety?

I will discuss in more detail in a future chapter about LifeVantage or Protandim. What I will say here is there are three key factors in helping you and your anxiety.

1 – Sleep. Everything comes from this. You don't sleep; you don't function. You lose control over you. You allow your anxiety centre stage, as an example, one night without sleep takes three days for the body and mind to recover as it needs to process all the information during the day and file all of your experiences. You need a structure and a pattern where you go to sleep every night. It needs to be a ritual every day, focusing on getting you the best sleep possible. I would include using a gratitude journal and cutting back on caffeine past four o'clock.

2 – Energy levels are a key component. Having the energy to keep going every day will give you more strength, build your confidence and give you the opportunity to be happier in your life. You will do the things you love doing. With energy levels beyond the level you have had for a long time!

3 – Focus. Mental strength will give you the ability to manage your emotions. Be clear and driven to realise your purpose. Your life dreams. You can do this through mediation. By appreciating the world. Linked to energy levels and nutrition, getting the right foods into your body will give you better clarity and strength in managing your anxiety.

This Chapter in a Nutshell

- Biohacking refers to the ability to hack your body through diet, rewiring your brain and supplements.

- Anyone can *Hack* their bodies!

- There are many forms of biohacking your body. Some will be too complicated to do here and some just won't be relevant, so I have split it up into two key areas mind(focus) and body (nutritional and energy levels). We will look at hacking our bodies through nutrigenomics and diet.

- Having a food journal is a key step to help you see how you eat.

- Sleep is another cornerstone of improving your anxiety.

- As anxiety sufferers we struggle with energy levels, there are many ways we can improve our levels.

Journaling

'Pour your heart out, let it all out, let it go.
Feel the pain and joy. Appreciate what is important.
Allow the mind to let all your problems go.'

What's in This Chapter?

Here you will learn how to hack your brain by focusing on what's important. Journaling is much underused form of hacking. Your brain has what I call the rehearsal loop. It means that until something that your brain feels is important to sort, it won't let go. It's constantly going around and around in your head. It either has to be done or written where the mind can then forget as it's not needed anymore. If it isn't dealt with, then this leads to a lot of stress and anxiety.

Journaling is the ability to pour your heart out onto a page, let it all come out, then think about how to either do it better next time or just leave it as that.

What Are the Benefits?

Journaling is an important process for us anxiety sufferers. It will aid in your sleep and in understanding your struggles, patterns, habits and behaviours. You can see it in a dispassionate perspective.

When Should I Journal?

I would recommend at the end of the day. This links well with sleep. It allows all your worries and fears to let go. Make sure you've structured it and have a clear positive focus. You can do it at the start and at the middle of the day if you wish. But do it before you go to bed.

How Will You Feel Afterwards?

Purging my soul has always been, for me, a positive change. It takes a huge weight off of my shoulders. I feel a sense of elation. I feel in control, empowered, calmer and considerably happier.

By doing this last thing at night, you will find a lot of worries, fears and concerns will be removed. Your mind literally forgets the problems. It's written, so why do you need to worry? You will also see what your mind-your thoughts are telling you.

I intend, when I get a little older, to give my journals to my daughter to read. So she can see my struggles and what I did about it.

You can do a journal in two ways. Structure it and take it from my book below. Or you can do your own ones that suits you.

What three things are you most grateful for today?

What has been your main emotion today?

What can you do differently tomorrow?

What did you enjoy most about your day?

What has been your biggest learning?

This Chapter in a Nutshell

- Journaling is a simple, easy and cool hack to refocus your mind. To see what your thoughts say.

- You can do this whenever you want but YOU MUST do it at night to aid your sleep.

- Journaling allows you to release your anxiety and stress by saying how you feel. Your mind naturally switches off a lot of the problems it feels you have dealt with.

- This isn't about ignoring a huge problem. Journaling won't help you hide the truth. More, to focus on what is important and to see patterns about yourself dispassionately.

- You feel calmer, happier. Like a weight has been taken off of your shoulders and aids in improving your sleep.

Hacking Your Brain!

'*What a change I have made to my life!
I feel alive, inspired. My anxiety has gone from
a scream to a whimper. I am in control, and I
will show the world what I am capable of!*'

What Is in This Chapter?

This is a fresh look at the brain. What I want to do is show you that your brain can be changed, adapted and trained to behave in a different way. The key is for you to be the conscious maker of change. We will show you tools you can use and insights in to what is possible. What you can do to make a change.

The human brain is an amazing supercomputer. Since the moment you were born your brain has inherited and learnt exact ways to behave and do it with the simplest of ease.

Allowing your conscious brain to focus on the more important things. We are constantly learning and adapting. The only problem is that sometimes our behaviour isn't right. As an adult, we have the power to change this. Sometimes we aren't even aware that our behaviour is wrong. For example, I have noticed a few times recently that I have been stressed and taking it out on my family. Not till I have meditated later in the day have I seen that I am stressed and or anxious. This isn't a high-level stress, this is the small, under-the-surface stuff. It is something I am working on to improve myself. But I wasn't aware I was doing it.

As anxiety sufferers, there are times during our day we too behave in a certain way. We kick in to survival mode. Our perception of the world is off. WE don't realise it. Then we behave in a way to push people off or be stressed, and we are surprised by the reaction of other people. Thinking the behaviour that is wrong is them. Truth is it isn't!

I want to teach you how to focus for longer. To manage your stress levels. To be calmer and to have tools/skills to understand your pains, roadblocks and to know what to with it when they appear. I want to give you the skills to rewire your brain. So you are not constantly in survival mode. To feel that you are in control of your life and not just coasting along with no clear direction and feeling trapped in the mind you are in.

Like I have lifted a weight from your shoulders. That you didn't even realise you had. To see that you are happy. To feel more confident as you can see the progress, your mind is making. To feel FREE! Free from the shackles of anxiety.

What We Will Focus On?

- Attention or focus

- Anxiety/worry

- Inspiration – throughout the book and this chapter

- Changing your perception/interpretations

- Your beliefs

- Your behaviours

- Self-care

- Journaling

Attention/Focus

You know the time when you feel like someone has control of your remote and you keep getting distracted. You know this job is important. But can you bloody focus on it?

Keeping you focused is a skill. It's a muscle you need to train and improve. I bet you can guess what the ways are for being more focused?

Meditation

Find a calm place. Breathe deeply but slowly. Allow your thoughts to come and go. Watch your thoughts, don't let them distract you. When they notice, then let go. I like to imagine your thoughts like balloons. Let them go. Watch them rise off into the distance.

Another way is to imagine thoughts as cars driving past you on a busy motorway. You know another will be past you in a second. The key is just to watch them. Not look inside, no judgement, no feelings, no fears. Just notice them. No need to react. The more you train yourself the easier it will be to be focused. So when you focus you will focus more. By watching your thoughts a key learning will happen.

I have spoken in some detail about this in both *Hope over Anxiety* and *Freedom over Anxiety*. However, it needs talking about again. Challenging your mind, your thoughts will see a massive shift in you. The chatter or what I describe it as just b*llsh*t. Constant, incessant cr*p that it's continually spouting! By seeing what your mind tells you, it will give you great knowledge, and great knowledge comes great power. I am sure I read that somewhere.

Focus

What you focus on is key to improving your anxiety. If you focus on the positive aspects of your life, you will see a notable shift in your perception. I find the happier I am, the better things happen. Because I am focusing on them.

This isn't about you ignoring the bad. You do need to look at that. But mentally focusing on the positive aspects of your life will encourage you to feel happier.

Look at it this way. Perceptions or more, your perceptions are key to what your mind focuses on. You only see around 20 percent of what is happening. Your camera lens is focusing on one thing. The brain does this because there is only so much it can see and take in. The rest we don't see. Essentially, you have a filter to your world that is going on. One incident someone will see a different way because their camera lens, their show, is on something else. This makes us unique but also leaves us to the mercy of our own perceptions of what is happening. You want a negative world? Focus on the negative and you will. Focus on the positive more, and you will have more positive experiences. They can make even the bad more bearable.

Ask yourself what can I learn from this? What else does this mean? It's about moving your focus from the emotional side of your brain to the more analytical human side. This will change your thought process attributed to the incident and your focus.

Be Kind to Yourself

You are doing your best. Understanding why, training your mind and putting tools in place are the key steps you need to manage the situation. Feeling overwhelmed and stressed will only mean that you will feel worse, lose control of what you are doing and give up. This is training a muscle and this takes time. Show compassion. It's about slowly improving yourself.

Understanding Why You Are Being Distracted

Giving goldfish a run for their money; According to a 2015 study from *Microsoft* have proven we have an attention span of just eight seconds! Your brain decides on what is important. If you work on your focus, you can last for longer.

Preparing Your Brain

Something I feel is important. I talk myself through what needs doing. Why it's important. I also ensure that to do my best work. I ensure the conditions to do so are perfect. So, for example, when I write. I find a quiet place. I lock myself away. Make sure everyone knows I won't be distracted. I hate it when I am. I am sure I am grumpy or I give death stares when I am. But this is when I can get in to full flow. When I can focus completely.

Preparing your brain, you need to get calm. Explain to yourself why you are doing it. What is the importance? So for me. I am determined to launch eight to ten books in about eight months. I want to be a full-time author. Which will mean I can help many more people more quickly. Get clear on what you want to do and what the benefit is to you and your loved ones.

If you need to meditate for two minutes or listen to music, then do so. You do your best work when you are in your calmest state. It's not winding yourself up. Making you stressed to do it. It's not about leveraging your anxiety. This is about calming yourself to get the best from you.

Your Beliefs

We went through this at the start of the book. I would like to elaborate a little more here. Your mind perceives what is happening to the world through your beliefs, what is right what is wrong. Our perceptions are not always correct, and there are beliefs we carry around that we have either taught ourselves or noticed from others.

One example is that for me to become the person I want to be: successful, wanting to help hundreds of thousands of people, has to mean great, painful, sacrifices. Has to mean a huge cost. It has to mean that I need to be grumpy and not willing to let anyone on the journey. In a nutshell, I have to be miserable! That's a ridiculous belief! To be my best me I have to be horrible to reach it? The pain has to be to the point of suffering for my art? Really?!

The reason I have that strange belief is that I have done this in the past, and in my perception, it has worked because I reached the end goal I wanted. BUT there was a cost to that. A huge one. There is another way. I have to catch that story now. As I don't want to be that person anymore. I want to have a new belief. One I can already have all I want without the pain. I can feel successful and happy. Time will bring me to my goals.

A Few More Beliefs That Just Aren't True

In order for me to be my best me, I have to be so kind and considerate, I don't consider my own feelings. That my negative feelings are gone. Rubbish!

I will not break anxiety because I am not strong enough to carry this burden anymore?

Come on, admit it? Have you ever said this story to yourself? The story is only true when you believe what you are telling yourself! You already have the strength, courage and will in spades. If you didn't you wouldn't be around now. All you have to do is apply that will to beating anxiety.

What Are Your Beliefs That Just Aren't True?

Write a few down here . . .

How Do You Break Them?

Write the old belief, how it has helped you and how it has made you feel. It has benefited you in the past sometimes but mostly not. You need to be as negative as you can. Feel the emotions of what you are writing. Now write your new belief and how it will feel when it works. How it will help you and how it will affect your loved ones around you.

Your Behaviours

Most behaviours you don't realise that you have. By meditation and writing behaviours you will see you from a different perspective!

You are in a constant state of healing. There are things I am still working on. It's about moving up the levels and understanding to get to the next step that you have to achieve and understand certain things.

I have found loads of roadblocks and problems I didn't know I was facing. Even now. That I am not aware of. Months. But every so often life shines a light on the issue. It gives you an a-ha moment.

There are times I have felt stressed and thought *why am I stressed? what is the problem?*

My biggest challenge over the next year is getting my behaviours right. Why do I need to improve my behaviours? There is a great saying that many high-thought leaders like to say. 'Who do you have to be?' To be the person you want. I see people I admire and take parts of their personality and adapt those traits into my personality.

I do this because, to move up the levels in my life, I need to be different to achieve. I want people to see me as a calm, curious, compassionate, caring, kind and full of fun. I want to do this naturally. I want it to be my authentic self. Not an act. I want people to be inspired by who I am and what I have done to get here.

My 'role' models have changed massively over the last two years. I shall write my role models now. Compare them to my first book *Hope over Anxiety*. There has been a massive change since it was written

ROLE Models Now and Why?

Jesse Elder – He is calm and full of knowledge. He has loads of courses I plan on doing over the course of the next year. From sleep upgrades, self-confidence and meditation. How he is with people is how I want to come across.

Rich Litvin – Calm, kind and caring. He coaches people so powerfully. He has brought me to tears how powerfully he helps people. Master of coaching and one I am keen to learn more from his courses. Willing to share his own vulnerability. Which I always have maximum respect for. It's a courageous and inspiring thing to do and totally respect anyone that is confident enough to share their own vulnerability.

Adam Croft – He is a *New York Times* best-selling author. His books have made over 1.5m sales! He has loads of knowledge. His mindset to his books, treating it like a business, I am totally intrigued by. I am fascinated to learn more as I continue my author journey. He is the level I want to be at.

Why Do You Need Role Models for Behaviours?

So I can learn from them and incorporate that in to me. If they consistently show what I am lacking, I can see what I need to do. I find that this in turns creates a problem of how do I show up in this manner? Using my structure during the day is integral to that.

I want to be clear this isn't about comparing myself to others. It is about either taking parts of their personality and making it part of me or learnings from them. I don't aim to be a clone of someone else. I aim to be a much better version of myself, and I use them to learn how to grow more for myself. For the people that love me.

Comparing isn't the right way to go. This may seem a little odd to say here, but I think it's massively important to understand that I am not after cranking my anxiety up, making myself feel inadequate. I am on my journey.

The higher up the ladder you go, the fewer people are on it. The fewer people will understand what you are doing, who you are becoming and why you are doing it.

I have had loads of criticism over the course of the last year. Some very unpleasant to the comical. I have also had thousands upon thousands of positive feedback. But I am thankful for the criticism. I am thankful that people don't believe in me and aren't supportive. Because it has made me driven. It has instilled in me an unbreakable belief I will achieve the goals I have set out for myself. People tell me that you haven't done it in the past so why do it now? You have never been successful. I smile knowing that they are wrong. Nothing will stop me from being the person I dream of being. Of where I want to take myself and my family.

One of My Biggest Challenges

I have found a challenge, a dilemma recently. I want to be this calm, almost serene person. Understanding that life will throw challenges. You will find struggles, but that is okay. But that contradicts what I have to be as a store manager. Basically, the person I am becoming means I am no longer very good at my job. I have had to make some big reflections and changes to how I am. Almost going backwards in my day job. I have to use a lot more anxiety, be harder on myself, able to expend a lot more energy. I almost feel like I have to go back to being like a headless chicken. I also have to change, albeit slightly, how I approach people and staff. With more urgency and a little less calm. I am hating it!

Which has brought up again my big fear of going back to the old me, pre-armed robbery? The lazy, poor me, I am a victim, never willing to finish things off. Not having the determination to get what's important done. Not able to appreciate the people I love. Not able to stop and understand the joy of life. The anxiety-fueled, depressed and lonely person I was. I don't want to step back into those shoes. I don't want to accept going backwards. Even a drastic fall back like that. I have learnt a behaviour that doesn't allow me to drop back in to the old me. I have focused on the path ahead. I see things far brighter. This requires me to be more negative. How do I still be the same person I am now but also back to being excellent at my job?

So What Did I Do?

This required several calls with my life coach. But I basically now do 80 seconds to success as I get to work. This is an adaption of my 60 seconds to success from my *Freedom over Anxiety* book. Where I change my roles from father to store manager for example. I breathe in for five, hold that breath for five, then breathe out for a count of five. I talk to myself minutes before I get to work. I go through what I want to be when I get to work. What challenges I will face to be that person, but this was the important bit. For the extra 20 seconds. I did the why. Why am I doing this? What is the importance of it?

So for this it was I want to be calm, in control, driven and have a passion for what I am doing.

I have had to dig deep in to my past to realise the excitement and passion I used to have. I have used meditation. I am finding increasingly that by getting calm I can drop questions to my soul and get good clear answers. Giving me even greater focus and clarity to what I REALLY want.

My fear of falling back hasn't happened. It lifted a weight off my mind. One I hadn't realised I was carrying.

I brought up so many challenges as I want to be that calm person. I am frustrated in my job, but I am managing it well. I want to make the next leap. Why on earth would I want to jump backwards? But I appreciate how important my job is. Not just for me and my family but the team that is developing. My leap to do this full time wouldn't be possible if I didn't have a job and many people who rely on me.

How to Develop and Increase Self-awareness of Your Own Behaviours

I have four ways. I would recommend that you remove the emotion. Be as objective as you can. Look at it like it is someone else. This isn't an opportunity to beat yourself up. This is about finding ways to see your behaviours and improve them. The more objective and honest you can be the more beneficial this exercise is. The simplest and most effective are:

1. Mediate.

2. Write a journal.

3. Reflect every week.

4. Ask people that you love and trust for honest feedback.

Ways to Improve Your Behaviours?

1. Start by doing just one thing.

2. Start with a small challenge then grow it bigger.

3. Journal!

4. Have a plan.

5. Understand what your motivations are, and pack it full of emotion so you stay on track.

An Important Comment

Going from being full of anxiety to someone calmer and a person you want to be proud of, there are loads of stages of healing. Do not feel disheartened, don't feel down. You have learnt and have loads of experience that certain behaviours have worked. But they are part of the old you that you need to move away from. Life will show you these behaviours. It's up to you to fix them. I will constantly go on about life coaching because you will improve and see a lot more with their help. You will improve far more dramatically with their help than what you would do without. My last year has been exponential improvements. But the great thing is that I have so much more to learn and heal from. That's okay. Because that is all part of life's journey.

Self-Care

This is an important section of the book and needs plenty of time spent on it. By doing this, you will understand its importance. You see that you can build a better you on this foundation!

As an anxiety sufferer this is our hardest challenge. We can be so kind, compassionate, caring and understanding to everyone else except ourselves. To ourselves we are horrendous. We are impatient, every small human error is highlighted, regurgitated repeatedly. We are demanding and we forgive nothing. My advice always stays the same. Think of yourself like you do your best friend. Treat you like them. Every mistake, every worry, everything. Be kind, be understanding. This takes a conscious effort. You can use journaling to help you. Everything you do, show compassion. You will find the more you show this kindness, the more you grow your confidence. Which will quieten your anxiety? Increase your belief in yourself and the best bit you will feel happier!

You are doing your best. This is a journey, and that takes time. Each error and mistake can be learned and improved. It's okay to reflect on your performance. All I ask is that you don't get too caught up on the thinking.

Your compassion to yourself will then seep out into what you say to yourself. A key problem with anxiety. We are constantly asking our supercomputer questions. Like why I am useless?

Questions like that are loaded. Your brain may not answer straight away. But it will and will come up with every experience you ever had that proves you are. That time when you tripped up on the pavement and everyone laughed. That tenuous experience that wasn't really a mistake, but hell, we will make sure it feels like it is to prove that you is STUPID!

Asking the Right Questions!

This is like challenging your thoughts. When your mind comes up with rubbish, ask yourself is this true? I often come up with harsh comments, which is counterproductive, but it works for me. *Is this a productive use of my time?* I have caught myself giving my anxiety a hard time. Words like *'not this again shut up!'* aren't helpful they are destructive. For you to make the change, you have to come across as kind and compassionate. In all parts of your life. Including your thoughts.

I have learnt that saying *'what does this mean?'* A good one to ask. Gets my analytical side out and removes the emotion from the situation. It desensitises the problem.

Stopping You from Crashing into Roadblocks

Crashing into roadblocks is part of self-care and it is so easy to get overwhelmed. I am juggling so much at the moment: The struggle of being a good father, being good at my job (very challenging when all I want to do is write and help people), being a good husband and pushing my author and life coaching.

I have learnt that if I have a clear focus on what I need to do. Constantly reviewing my progress, praise and rewarding myself when needed and asking myself how will I achieve this? What do I need to do to make this happen? When there are challenges that get in the way and prevent me from getting to my goals, has kept me focused. There are so many opportunities to be ambushed. I want to improve my book's sales; I want to write another book; I am so excited about writing my first fiction book. I want to improve my email list; I need to send that message to Laura; I need to reply to X I haven't sent a post today that needs sorting. I ask myself three questions?

Is it urgent for my main goal? Releasing a book?
Is it relevant?
Is it important?

That way I can group them into importance. When I hit a problem, my mind doesn't want me to go forward. I ask myself a simple question; how much do you want to be a full-time author and help others? What will happen if you don't? How will it feel if you do? I make sure I describe how it will feel. How special it will be. Then I ask myself do you want to throw this away? All you have to do is this today.

Feelings

If I can describe the positive emotions will have on me and get as detailed as possible I have found it highly motivational. I have found that if I keep making these moves towards my big goal, I feel far happier in myself and that comes out to others.

I love writing. Putting words down on a page really fills me with joy. I have now formed a habit every day doing it. It has taken me a long time to get to the point and finding it in my structure to my day. (Originally it was first thing in the morning but it ended up waking my son up too early and making me feel too tired!) Knowing I am hitting my goals fills me with pride and when I tell people I will write three books in four months they are surprised, shocked and show a lot of respect for doing it. That gives me the heart I am doing it. I have constant reminders I am progressing. From my word count to seeing the book growing into something awesome. Loving the development of the book.

What Does This Mean to You?

By FEELING what you need to do by understanding what your purpose is, your goals and constantly reviewing them will give you hope, courage, determination and above all else happiness. It does me.

Keep Raising the Bar

By continuing to hack your brain to push YOU beyond what you ever felt possible, you will see (I would recommend journaling here) the progress you are making. You will see so many positives. Keep all of them. Review them when you need some courage or when you are feeling down. It will give you heart and reignite your courage. Confidence in YOU is key to self-care and breaking anxiety.

Raising the bar also has an important back stop. That is don't fall back. Your bar is raised as is your standards. Do not allow yourself to fall back in to the old you. What I do is I ask myself if I want to go back to the old me. I find that extremely motivating. I still fear the old me. I am working on it, but it's something I don't want to happen. So the bar has to be moved up every single day. Meaning I have more distance from that person. Again, you see you are making considerable progress. This is about acceptance. What you accept and what you don't. The line you never go back to. The bar goes up higher so does your acceptance levels for what you want to become.

You are constantly changing. None of us are stuck. That's the amazing thing about life. You can choose whatever you want to be.

Failure Is an Option!

Fear is the biggest part of anxiety and doesn't come as potent as the fear of failure. In any form. Even the tiniest, smallest mistakes are highlighted 10 million percent by us. Because we are so aware of our own errors and not wanting to feel any more of a failure than what we already are. We tend to go for the safest option most of the time.

I openly encourage pushing yourself and willing to make mistakes. The ability to go for things and get things wrong brings a great deal of learnings. I have achieved so much the last two years. I have also failed spectacularly too. But it has given me great lessons that have improved myself and the way forward.

Two Examples

Spending a great deal on advertising on Facebook with advertisements, I had thousands of people view my videos and hundreds of comments. But I was after people wanting help with their anxiety so I could coach them one to one. I poured all my effort in to learning how to create clients and help others, except really that wasn't what I wanted. Not completely. It is something I want to continue, but it's not my major focus and the thing I get the most pleasure from at the moment. That's the joy of writing, the feel of pouring my heart out to inspire others, I love doing it. Without putting too much time in to life coaching I wouldn't have learned the right mindset I needed to become a full-time author. I wouldn't have reflected on my performance up to August and thought. This isn't working. What do I need to do so I achieve my goal? I want to be a full-time author, I then want to improve my life coaching. But being a full-time author is the most important. What do I have to do to make that possible? How can I achieve that? What obstacles will I face? How do I get round them?

Focusing Too Much on My Books

Many people would agree that it is an obsession with me. It's all I talk about. I want to be the most knowledgeable about what places to market my book. What's the simplest way of launching a book? What is the right mindset? I also want to achieve this in a lot less time than others. My mistake is allowing it to be all I focused on. Allowing my impatience to keep my anxiety up. Meaning I became distant, driven, not open to talk to my family. Focusing all the time I had outside my job on achieving it. I know that long term I will achieve it and it will be worth it, BUT! The sacrifices aren't worth it. I have learnt that I need to invest time with my family and cut back on what I am doing. Now I am not juggling things. I have cut back on

Facebook. I am not saying YES! To everything that comes my way.

I have said this in my previous book *Hope over Anxiety,* but my journey is important. I want to show the world, my family and myself what is possible. I get tunnel visioned and shut off. I do not want to be doing so well in my career, helping so many but not having the people that matter the most by my side. It would mean sh*t if I didn't have it.

I have had to relearn this experience again and again. It seems each time something changes. But the basics remain the same.

The first step is accepting you have failed. To reflect on it to see what has happened. But not to see it as a failure. Failure is integral to my development. Fear holds us back so much. It's worrying about the worse that will happen if I do it. I see the feeling of fear. That knot in your stomach, the shaking, the shallow breathing, the worry as a barometer. I want to do this. I have tamed my fears many times. I know that I can overcome them. What will happen if I fail? Would it really be as bad as you fear it will be? Honestly? Ninety-nine point nine percent it isn't. It's that small, tiny chance it could be terrible! I know that it's just my fear. I now have that power over it and can push through. Because of my bloody mindedness but also I have built up evidence and have a total conviction that anxiety is a liar. Even if you fail what can happen? Learn from the mistake and move on.

I bet you have learned the old saying about Thomas Edison and the light bulb. He 'failed' 1,000 times before he found how to do it. He got asked why did he not give up. His response was I have learned how not to do it. Each time I experiment I learn something new.

I am getting there but I see life as a game. If you tackle it with a sense of joy, curiosity and compassion you won't be far off.

How would you like to live your life? Act on your fears. Every time you feel real fear, anxiety and worry. Do what is panicking you the most! Each time you win. Either way. You get it wrong, you see that the worse didn't happen. You see what your anxiety is doing. You quieten your fears. You understand how important perseverance is and the willingness to f*ck up. I am becoming an expert at it. With each level up the challenges become bigger and the f*ck ups potentially greater. But don't let your fears hold you back from the person you can be!

Chapter in a Nutshell

- Our brain is an amazing supercomputer that is constantly learning and adapting. Us anxiety sufferers struggle with getting stuck in survival mode. The place our brain keeps us so ensure we are safe.

- What you focus on during your day will happen. WE create our own worlds by what our eyes or our lens focuses on. If you want a better life you need to change what you focus on.

- Be kind and understanding to yourself. You are doing your very best. So don't be so hard on yourself. You need to be kind and compassionate. Treat yourself how you would treat your best friend.

- Our beliefs dictate with where you can take your life what you can achieve with anxiety and how you feel. If you believe you won't beat anxiety. You won't.

- Who are your role models? Who are the people you can learn from how they present themselves and how they are?

- There are four simple ways to improve your own awareness of your behaviours. They are mediation, journaling, reflecting, asking for feedback from people you love and trust.

- Improving your behaviours need you to start with just one small thing, start with one small challenge then grow it bigger, journaling, have a plan, understand what your emotions are and pack it full of emotion so you stay on track.

- Asking yourself the right questions is important to change your focus and to challenge your thoughts.

- Never accept the old standards! That comes from the old you. Keep raising the bar. Strive to do better every day. Even one percent will have a dramatic impact on your life.

- Be prepared to fail. Failure is such a key part of learning. We should embrace it. Some of my greatest achievements have come from failure.

Why Sleep Is So Important

'The alarm sounds. I feel alive. My anxiety is under control I feel happy. Excited to take on the day and looking forward to my next adventure. What can today bring? Can't wait to find out!'

What Is in This Chapter?

We will go through the stages of sleep. We will go through ways of helping you improve your sleep. Including your day-to-day activities. We will go through how important and integral sleep is to your overall well-being. Without a proper sleep every night you will not beat anxiety. It is a cornerstone of a better life and less anxiety.

What I will stress is that sleep does not start when you want to go to sleep. Sleep starts the minute you wake up in the morning. Everything you do during your day will decide whether you have a good night sleep. Too much caffeine you find yourself up too much using your anxiety. You sat on your phone for too long or you've been using it before you go to bed. Eating too many sugary foods during the day and before you go to bed. You have not meditated. These are examples what you need to make sure you manage during your day. Want a good night's sleep? Want to understand what sleep's all about and why it's so important? Want to understand how you can have a better night's sleep? What the impact you can have on your anxiety? Then this chapter is for you!

Zzzzzzz

Regular sleep seems, for most anxiety sufferers, unattainable. It seems to be no matter how hard you try, no matter what time you go to bed, you still don't sleep when you get there.

By using a few simple hacks, you will have a much better sleep. Imagine waking in the morning, sun beating down on your face, you stretch your body and a smile on your face. You don't feel groggy; you don't feel grumpy; you feel happy and excited for the day without the worry of anxiety.

Fact: More than 40 million Americans suffer from chronic long-term sleep disorders.

The Health Risks

Inadequate sleep can lead to poor performance at work or at school, increased risk of serious health issues and other health problems. Not mentioning anxiety, mood disorders and depression.

Most people with sleep disorders have a higher risk of heart disease, heart failure, irregular heartbeats, heart attacks, high blood pressure, stroke, diabetes and obesity.

researching yourself. There are a whole host of trials that have been proven that it works!

What Is NRF2?

Also known as the yellow pill, it reduces inflammation and increases your energy levels. I have seen a dramatic improvement in what I can do in a day now.

It has five herbal extracts, and it activates the NRF2 pathway. It aids your body to produce enough enzymes to reduce the main malfunctions the body has.

What Are the Benefits?

There are extensive testimonials on what this yellow pill has done for them.

The results range massively. From people that have struggled after strokes and traumatic brain injuries survivors to people that have improved from cancer.

NRF2 can help you become focused on what you are doing. Enabling you have a lot more energy. I have a strenuous and busy job that requires me to carry heavy stock around, manage my team and manage my customers. My level of progress inside of my job and out of it has been dramatic. It has also reduced my anxiety. One crazy yellow pill a day, taken with your breakfast.

What It Does?

- Drastically reduces cellular stress

- Helps to upregulate your survival genes

- Helps the body repair and rejuvenate its own cells

- Aids the body in detoxify genes, keeping the body's master blueprint of the cells function intact.

What Does That Mean for You?

It would mean being able to take on your anxiety, feeling the best you have ever felt. Even without the added chapter that will aid your recovery these two pills will make a life changing impact on your life. More energy, reduction in aches and pains, and more focus for longer. Whatever you are focusing on.

What Does This Mean?

Cardiologist Dr Benedict Maniscalco describes this best, he said when you combust petrol, hydrogen is produced. When you combust oxygen, free radicals are produced. Your body removes these. However, as you age your body slows up production and the ones you have slow down in their efficiency. Allowing the free radicals to attach themselves to parts of your body. This is cellular aging. What this magic pill does is ramp up production and activate the body. This SLOWS down the aging process and all the things that come with it. There are over 200 different illness, diseases, etc. Linked to cellular aging.

Here are just a few of them:

- Cancers

- Hepatitis B

- Heart disease

- Kidney damage

- Fatigue

For each day you go without proper sleep, it takes three further days for the mind and the body to fix the damage that's done. I lose memory or important pieces of information.

Sleeping is oh so much more than sleep. It has been scientifically proven that a big problem you have is better and is worked out by the brain whilst you sleep.

An example a violinist struggling with a new piece of music, will find they're able to play it better after a night sleep, as a brain is going through it and learning what has happened over the day.

You should never give up sleep to sort a problem. The brain is doing this whilst you sleep.

The 4 Steps of Sleep

I find the process of how our minds and bodies sleep fascinating. I will go into more detail on this. It's important to understand the process, so that you can see why sometimes you wake up groggy or how important it is to go to sleep and wake up at the same times. There are several times our bodies go into a deep sleep. This cycle ranges in times. There are two main parts of the cycle, REM or rapid eye movement and non-REM, non-rapid eye movement. Make sense? There are a few myths that you don't dream during non-REM, this isn't true. Sleep takes you on a repetitive peaks and troughs with some of the journey being wild! According to studies,75 percent of your sleep cycle is in non-REM and 25 percent in REM. There are periodic cycles of this during the night.

Non-REM has four stages. During a typical night we go through stages of non-REM, and REM, then back through the non-REM stages again. It repeats this cycle every 90 minutes.

Stage 1 – Transitional sleep lasts normally only a few minutes. This is the lightest stage of sleep. Highest chance of you getting woken up is at this stage.

Stage 2 Slightly deeper than stage 1, usually lasts 5 to 15 minutes.

Stage 3 Eye and body movements reduce down dramatically.

Stage 4 Deepest stage of sleep. Usually the first time this cycle starts lasts around 20 to 40 minutes.

The cycle then drops back into stage three to two. This lasts ten to fifteen minutes. Then going into a surprise period of REM sleep. As the night progresses there is a reduction in non-REM sleep. Half of the night's REM sleep is during the final third of your sleep. The longest REM period is between 30 to 50 minutes. This then goes into 30 minutes of non-REM sleep before going back into REM sleep.

The average night sleep for most people should be seven and a half hours sleep.

During REM the body shuts down with only the eyeballs and breathing being active. Dreaming is strong.

What Impact Does This Have on You?

Understanding the process between how your sleep works will give you knowledge of how your brain works. Meaning you will understand why you struggle or feel groggy when you are interrupted during your sleep.

Ways to Get a Better Night's Sleep – Structure

Your mind needs to have a structure for its day. You will need to become calm, you need to cut back on caffeine. Having at least three times during your day for yourself. This is in an important point and needs repeating: if you are constantly in anxiety mode and you find that sleep will not come when you want it, because your mind is still racing, it is important to rest your brain at least three times a day. It does not have to be for a long time. Having these three times of rest will reset your brain and keep you calmer.

I would prefer that you meditate, but it doesn't have to be meditation. This is an alone time for yourself quiet time. Your mind needs this. I talk more about this in my second book *Freedom over Anxiety*. What is important to say here is that you need to have habit, rituals to your day. You do them every day, without fail. It is part of who you are. You can customise what you need to do to aid you. This is your life, your mind. You are the expert on what works best for you.

If Not Meditation, What?

Here are a few examples that I use. There are many others, but these ones work for me.

You can use this alongside, or instead of, meditation.

OmHarmonics

I have talked about this in my recent book *Freedom over Anxiety,* but it is an excellent alternative to meditation. One thing I will point out is it works best for me when I am already stressed getting annoyed, getting angry or getting worried. I have found it less when I'm in my calm, happy state. It is different to meditation in that you can listen to it putting the washing out or taking the dog for a walk. All you need is your headphones and searching for it on YouTube. Unlike meditation, you don't have to work on calming yourself. Rather, the music itself will get you into your calmest most blissful state, naturally, without the need to focus on it.

Music

Find music you find calming, music that brings you joy, that brings a tear to your eye, that allow you to escape. Listen, allow the music to wash over you. Let YOU feel it.

Reading

For me, it does two things, and I am sure it will do the same for you. Firstly, it will naturally get you into a calm state. Secondly, whatever the book you're reading allows you to escape and see the world from a different angle. Make sure you enjoy reading this book regardless of what it is. Reading can shine a light on how you are feeling, speak your world you weren't even aware of, see it in a different way and will expand your Horizons.

Sleep (Again!)

Sleep time needs to be consistent every night. Going to bed at very similar times and getting up similar times is imperative. You have an internal body clock, sticking to this will allow you and your brain to know when it's time for bed and to switch off. This may seem a simple point so many people miss it.

Many phones have reminders of when you need to go sleep. I use this. I have a 15-minute timer before eight hours. This allows me to get myself ready to take my NRF1 pill and put my meditation on. Naturally, as you get more in to a settled routine, your body will tell you that you are tired and ready for sleep.

If you want to take on anxiety and beat it, learn how to get a good night sleep. It is one cornerstone of breaking anxiety. Without it, you won't do it as your mind, body and emotions will be all over the place. Your anxiety will have a field day! Loving the chaos!

Starting Your Day

With mindfulness I would highly recommend for you even get out of your bed to meditate. This only needs to be for a maximum of five minutes. Find something inspiring to rev up your day, put you in the right frame of mood.

Breakfast

They say the breakfast is the most important meal of the day. I totally agree with this. So I highly recommend having a good breakfast not a full English (Bacon, sausage, toast that sort of thing) to kick start your day. Also, for breakfast I would have my NRF2 supplement.

Five Minutes Stop Anyone?

Time out, focus on your breathing, allow the world to carry on for just five minutes whilst you spend time with your mind and your breath.

Dinner Time!

I am always on the run so I grab a sandwich. I have found that I love eating tuna sandwiches. Great brain food. Grab something healthy and substantial to keep you going then stop and meditate or get calm, whatever works best for you.

4pm and Above

Swap out your caffeinated drinks for green teas. They have excellent health benefits. Reducing the caffeine content is imperative. Caffeine lasts for a long time in your system and you will still have over 25 percent of it in your body the following day. Too much caffeine keeps your mind active and cannot sleep. I highly recommend avoiding energy drinks ever. Especially after 4pm I'll probably go as far as say not to drink after 12pm because these are high in sugar and caffeine. Caffeine mimics anxiety or, more correctly, the symptoms of anxiety.

You Are at Home, Time to Take the Dog for a Walk

What I like to do during the summer is I like going into the woods to take the world as it is. I watch my dog sniff around. I take deep, slow breaths and look at the beauty in the world. I watch the birds flying over my head. I see the sun setting with beautiful oranges and yellows over the sky. Setting the clouds alive with colour. I found this grounds me. In just 10 minutes of taking my dog for a walk I've reset my mind ready for the night ahead.

Watching TV

You can do this but please, please, please be careful what time you stop watching. Too much during the day will activate your brain and keep you awake just like watching it just as you go bed. I would advise at least 20 minutes before you hit the sack that you have stopped any technology.

Hitting the Sack

I highly recommend that you stop drinking any alcohol after 8 pm. I have experienced myself that I struggle to go to sleep. My sleep patterns are irregular, I am constantly waking up and I feel 10 times worse in the morning because I have no sleep and being constantly woken up. Alcohol is also a depressant.

I have talked about this in my previous two books *Hope over Anxiety* and *Freedom over Anxiety* so I won't go in to too much detail here. However, what we will talk to you about is the need to journal. Being able to put your feelings down onto a paper is important. Make sure it is in some structure. What I do is I ask myself three things I am most grateful for today and what did I enjoy most about today. What is my main goal for tomorrow? Any anxiety worries you have we write here to put a positive spin on or, else is a risk of you bringing up all your emotions from the day and making it impossible to sleep.

Some Good Examples of What You Should Put in Your Journal

What feelings did you have mostly during the day?

What are the 3 things that you are most proud of today?

What 3 things do you appreciate most today?

What is your main goal you want to achieve tomorrow?

Then it's time for bed. Put the meditation on. You can have the same one on every night or mix it up. I have found that repeating the same meditation has meant that within minutes of putting it on, I am falling asleep!

This Chapter in a Nutshell

- Your sleep can be influenced from the minute you wake up!

- Eight hours seems to be the myth, but on average you should sleep around seven and a half hours. I struggle with anything less than eight.

- Sleep has many stages. From non-REM to REM. The stages are intertwined. Where the body drops quickly from transitional sleep, to light sleep then moving between for most of the night from REM to non-REM. Starting the first part of the night 10 to 20 minutes finishing at the final third from 30 to 50 minutes.

- Having a structure to your day is integral to getting a good night sleep.

- Not having enough sleep has short-term and long-term effects on your mind, body, emotions and anxiety.

- Without proper sleep you have no chance of breaking anxiety.

- Keeping calm and not worrying is integral to a good night sleep. You can do this by reading, listening to your favourite music, OmHarmonics and meditation.

- Make sure you have a routine where you go sleep and wake up roughly the same time every day.

- Make sure you journal, meditate and take your NRF1 before you go sleep. I prefer the same meditation on every night as it encourages me to know when it's time for bed.

When Nature Calls!

'The sun sets in yellows, blues and oranges. I breathe in. I watch the trees sway to the wind. The flowers in bright colours. I focus on my breath and breathe out. Such beauty. My sanctuary and my escape from my hectic life. My time to appreciate. To slow down.'

What Is This Chapter About?

This is about showing you how to appreciate the world you have. How to get your own headspace and understand the benefits of being at one with nature and how that can help you. I will also add a little of structure to encourage you to make this a habit.

As an introvert I can't recommend doing this enough. I take my dog for a walk. It's a chance to escape the busyness of the world. Not to be hassled or any demands on you. I get such small time to get away, to escape it's important. I find this time. Every day!

Being out in the countryside, in the woods(forest) or appreciating the simple things in life. The bloom of a flower, for example, has grounding benefits for you. To see the world for what it is. To get out of your own head.

A key thing is that you don't have to be deep in the forest. It can be the woods. It can be in your own garden if you have plenty of green. This is about finding a sanctuary. It is another excellent tool to use. You need loads of sanctuaries, I do, during my day. This will allow you to recharge or even reflect. It gives you so many opportunities to shut off.

What Are the Benefits?—How Will You Feel Afterwards?

Calm, I can ground myself in the moment. I feel that it is my reset. My chance to get calm ready for the busy evening of jobs. To help me realise how small I am and how much beauty there is in the world. I make sure I touch the forest. Especially if there is a poppy swaying in the wind. I love the feel of flowers. The soft but strong leaves. It may be as I am a little weird.

There is a fascinating article. That I want to prove my point, from mindful—one of my favourites. The article is called *Why Forest Bathing Is Good for Your Health*. It is taken from Qing Li's new book, *Forest bathing: How Trees Can Help You Find Health and Happiness*. In it they describe an extensive study done on 'Forest bathing'. Yes, really! There is really a thing! Forest bathing isn't about running naked through the forest. It is about walking and absorbing the calm. Watching mother nature. Centering yourself and appreciating the amazing beauty that surrounds us. It originates from Japan and they call it shinrin yoku.

In it I learned some amazing information. You have more benefit in the forest in the afternoon. Than you do in the morning.

The study by Li discovered walking in the forest can:

- Reduce anxiety

- Improve people's vigor

- Reduce fatigue

- Reduce depression

- Reduce anger

- Improve the immune system

- Boost overall well being!

Another of Li's studies discovered that it can also improve sleep patterns. They discovered that they slept better, for longer and became less anxious.

So taking time outs from your day to see the world can have a serious improvement in your mental and physical health.

Seriously? How Is That Even Possible?

There is a study that to improve your creative skills and help people feel calmer you need to wear green or have green in your offices and home. Some suggest that we are hardwired to connect with nature. It has a positive effect on the health of us humans.

You can incorporate walking which is an exercise that is important to form your own health. It has been shown to reduce anxiety, depression, blood pressure, etc. Using it to walk in nature will give you a further boost to your health.

Some Health Benefits

Being in the forest, you have an increase in oxygen. There are also natural oils from the plants defence system called phytoncides. They have apparently excellent benefits to us if we are exposed to them. Psychological stress is reduced and blood pressure and heart rate are lowered. Sounds like an excellent hack!

When Do I Do It?

I do two walks with my dog. One in the morning and one at night just as I have got home. I would suggest that you too should find an excuse to do similar. Even if you don't have a dog, ten minutes will dramatically influence your health. We are so busy. Just taking that time out will help you.

Is There Anything Special That I Need to Do?

Embrace it. Appreciate it for what it is. Understand that you will need this time. Just connect with nature. You can either find a place to appreciate it or walk around. Just make sure it has evergreens in it. Like pine, cedar, spruce and conifers to get the best benefits.

How Will I Feel Afterwards?

Feeling calmer, your blood pressure and heart rate are already naturally lower. Less anxiety and less depression. Able to connect with the world. Able to shut off. Feel free. Feel you are able to take on life again. Able to use this time to reflect. Some quiet time to fix a problem or just be.

Additional—Enjoying the Beach

You walk barefoot along the sandy beach. The feel of the sand on your feet. The slight lick of the warm breeze on your face. The sun is beaming. The sea rolls in gently. You breathe to the rhythm of the sea. The water laps around your feet. It feels cooling on a hot summer's day. You feel relaxed. You close your eyes and take it all in. The sun hits your face. You are alone, peaceful, bliss. In a blissful state of awareness. Heaven.

Just like forest bathing. Appreciating a beautiful summer's day by the sea has great healing powers too. It reduces your blood pressure; it aids in you feeling calmer; it aids your sleep. Pretty much everything we have discussed in this chapter. Being at the beach has similar benefits. So if being in the forest isn't your thing, then I would recommend enjoying the seaside instead.

This Chapter in a Nutshell

- Being in nature, I would highly recommend. Forest bathing is really a thing!

- According to studies, it has been proven to reduce fatigue, anxiety, depression and your blood pressure! There are other good health benefits of breathing in the highly oxygenated air.

- Find a time when it works for you. It need not be for too long. Ten minutes is enough. If you want to take your dog for a walk, then this will kill two birds with one stone.

- It has been found that going in the afternoon is more beneficial.

- You will feel calmer, less stressed, lower blood pressure, more invigorated and more energy.

Finding Your Bliss

'The headphones are on. The music plays and I can escape. I can feel the music. It's playing just for me. A wave of emotion comes over me. Joy, a release, tears fill in my eyes. The weight of the world has gone. I listen. I feel such beauty. I let myself go. Allow myself to be carried along by the soulful, beautiful music.'

What's in This Chapter?

A great tool, one I have recently discovered. I regularly listen to calm music to reduce stress now. This is something I know on my dinner break I can appreciate. I know that I have music I can get lost in. Allow all my fears, worries and stress to dissipate. Just to feel the music to get lost in the feelings. It regularly brings me to tears. I feel this is a cool hack to rewire your brain and to focuses you. I can tell you how blissful I feel listening to it.

What Are the Benefits of It?

Knowing that you have time during your day to completely get lost, to switch off and allow all your pains, fears worries to leave you. Having joy and happiness.

I love some classical music. I don't want to listen to words. I want to be swayed to the emotional connections of the songs. It allows me to slow up and just be present. I can also do other things when I am listening to it. Either writing this or doing jobs around the house.

So it's awesome for multi-tasking!

How Will You Feel Afterwards?

Calm, peaceful and mellow. Full of happiness. Like a huge weight has been removed from you.

Two Top Recommendations to Listen to

These are ones I love, however, you may not find these help. I would recommend having a little look through YouTube and finding a few.

Having this tool to use when you need it is empowering. This isn't about listening to angry music. This is about just opening up to yourself. Allowing your emotions to the surface and letting the music dictate to you how you should feel.

When Should You Listen to It?

It all depends on you. I find that most times I can listen to it. However, sometimes it only works when I am a little stressed beforehand. If I am calmer when I listen to it, I feel calmer. I still feel a sense of bliss whenever I listen.

This Chapter in a Nutshell

- Listen to calming music for stress. There are many types you can choose from.

- It puts you in a blissful state. I find it takes the weight of the world off of me. I find it simple and easy to do. All I have to do is totally listen and let my emotions come out. Be open.

- It's another great skill or tool to help you feel calm. An alternative to meditation, if you wish, or just as good alongside.

- You can do this either lying down with your headphones or whilst working around the house.

Meditation
and Your Anxiety

---

*'I breathe in. I feel calm. I am
compassionate to myself. It's okay to make
mistakes. It's okay being less than perfect. I am
happy in my skin. I like the person I am. I don't
react. I see my anxiety for what it is.'*

What Is in This Chapter?

I use meditation to calm my rapid 1000 miles an hour
brain. That is my biggest challenge. This manifests itself in
impatience and frustration. Being able to watch your
thoughts and feelings but able to not react to them is an
empowering experience.

It gives you the power back. I am getting close to the
golden figure and the expert's description of what mastery

is. Ten thousand hours of meditation coming up for almost a year meditating.

The Benefits of This Section

By the end of this step, you will see your thoughts and feelings like me and not react. You will feel empowered understanding that everyone has their own struggles and frustrations. You will feel 50 percent calmer. You will understand the massive importance of meditation.

Mindful meditation is the cornerstone of breaking anxiety. I can't recommend it enough. Through practice it allows you a space between your thoughts and feelings. Where you can react or not? It's a small space, but oh so important.

I have an end goal to the person I want to be. I want to be far calmer, far more compassionate and far more grateful.

I want to see more of this wise person. I get glimpses of when I meditate. He sees the chaos of life. Sees life as a game. Appreciates the beauty in the world. He is serene and happy. Not most of the time. But all the time.

Some stats about meditation. A study in the UK found that for each year that you meditate you remove one biological year from your life. That's right, you don't age as much if you meditate!

In 1978, Robert Keith Wallace study took blood pressure, eyesight and hearing. Comparing the scores of those tests to determine if there had been any improvement.

Not convinced yet about meditation? In the *Scientific American* a survey was carried out in November 2013. It learnt not only just meditation changes brain neural neuronal interconnections, but it increases brain tissue volume, decreases the volume of the amygdala which causes anxiety and reduces inflammation and other biological stresses.

Another study found that those that meditated for five years or fewer took five years of ageing from their biological age. For those that meditated over five years, twelve years were removed from the ageing. So a sixty-year-old would have the mind and body of a forty-eight-year-old.

From studies, meditation has been proven to reduce your anxiety by 50 percent in one month. If you do it for at least 15 minutes each day. From this section you will learn suggestions to add to your day. I will add this to your 7-day plan at the end of the book.

They will be simple and easy-to-use steps. That can easily be slid into your day. Either through stealth, where you can do it when no one notices, or via alone time where you can find time to meditate even if it is for five minutes. I disappear from work and get in my car. So that there aren't any interruptions.

I know that alone time is limited and precious so I will give you as many good ideas as possible.

A Key Point

Do you want to do this? If you don't believe it will work, or you aren't prepared to fight for that alone time, then you'll find you won't last long meditating. I would give you two weeks tops before you will stop. It has to be something that is imperative that gets done.

Don't worry if you struggle to meditate. I have another cool way of getting calm and meditating in a different way. I shall talk about this later.

How Does It Feel When Your Mind Is Calm?

You feel relaxed. You feel positive and hopeful. With more meditation you will feel more caring and compassionate of others. You will see a lot more what your mind says to you. You will notice a lot more patterns of behaviour and notice what you eat. Being able to spot these things will help you later in the book and help you become a far better, happier person.

I see my thoughts for what they are. I have a small space of time. So I can react to my thoughts or not. I can see what my thoughts are saying and don't react. I am in control of me. I manage my anxiety because I feel calmer. I feel more positive about myself and the world around me.

Some Basic Meditation Techniques – To Start a Fairly Easy One

Find somewhere that feels comfortable. I would recommend finding somewhere out of the way from distractions, a place you will use every time you want to meditate. This way it aids you in getting your mind focused. As your brain is already prepared for it as it associates this place with calm and your time. I find that my bed is my best place. Stare out into space. Take long deep breaths to this for a count of five then close your eyes.

All that is required for this meditation is to focus on your breath. To center you. Allow your breathing to go back to normal. For each in breath notice it and count one. Go to the count of ten. Then reset and start again. If your thoughts come to distract you it's okay. This is perfectly normal. Notice and let it go. By doing this, it will center you and aid in you being calmer. It will allow your mind to rest. You can do this for as long or short as you need. I personally would recommend five minutes minimum.

A Simple Technique 2—The Body Scan

Again find a quiet place. Preferably the same place. Keep your eyes open for a count of five. Take deep breaths during this time then close them. Allow your breath to return to normal. From the top of your head slowly go down from your head to the tip of your toes. Ask yourself how is the body feeling today? What are its aches and pains? What is the overall feel to the body today? Don't over analyse this. It is to note it. Not to do anything with that information, just be aware. No judgement, no criticism, just the thought. Being aware is healing. I recommend this is done for a minimum of two minutes. But you can decide when you feel it is enough.

There are thousands, upon thousands, of meditation techniques on the internet, I have pulled out a couple more. These are some I do myself.

Below are a couple of advanced forms:

Technique 3

The easiest one you can do EVER!

Put on a calm and stress free music on YouTube. Listen to it and feel it. Breathe normally. Just feel the music. Don't even need to be in your calm place. Do the washing. Put it on your headphones. I am listening to one now as I type.

Getting Answers to the Most Important Questions—Advanced Meditation

I have spoken about this a little way up the previous chapter. But it needs repeating and elaborating a little further. You have two types of thoughts. The chatter, the nonsense that is constantly spouting out of your mind. It rarely stops. This is where you can't forget that phone bill or anxiety is kicking in throwing sh*t at you.

But there is another train of thought. This wise, knowledgeable head. Behind the chatter. By meditating and asking myself important questions such as *What do you really want? Do you want to write or life coach? What is important to you?* The deep stuff that fuels us. That makes us happy. What we really want in our lives. Knowing these answers is powerful. To learn that we have those answers, and they aren't on far away distant land, has been such a joy and an important learning for me over the last six months. To know every single important question is deep in you, is sitting in your soul, all you have to do is ask and be quiet enough to hear it!

How Do You Do That?

Get quiet. Ensure you are in your favourite place when you are meditating. Breath in deeply. Do a body scan. Focus on your breath for at least five minutes. You must be in your calmest, most peaceful state. Because if you don't it won't be your soul you are talking to. But your chatter.

Ask it calmly. If there is no response, answer again. Be compassionate, kind and curious.

Recently I asked a question to myself. *What do I enjoy most about my day?* I could have responded, spending time with my children or wife. Nope! My answer was that I enjoyed sitting down with my cereal, smoothie and banana the most. I realised that as my morning is so manic. Getting my son and daughter, sorted and dog for a walk and myself sorted meant I didn't sit down for my breakfast, more I rushed it. Shoveling it in. So sitting down and eating it, appreciating the meal was my enjoy most. How fascinating!

Getting rid of the ego. A good friend of mine, Ayla Grace Zelles, a sex and relationship coach, taught me this.

I have explained in previous chapters, but like always it needs repeating. You have two thoughts. One is the chatter of the mindless rubbish that is constantly spouted out of your head and there is something higher. More spiritual, more enlightened. I feel it's my soul. My wise.

I find trouble being able to listen to my higher person. Because my ego is so bloody loud!

This technique will help you with that. ALSO another good thing—it requires only three minutes of your time a day!!

You can start this on one minute and build. There is a risk of you getting dizzy as you are quickly inhaling a lot of air. Maybe even feel a little drunk. Stop if that happens. You can build this up.

Ego Eradicator with a Breath of Fire

Sit crossed legged. With your back straight. Put out your arms up to 60 degrees above your head. Close your eyes and close your fingers to the palms of your hands. Leave the thumb out. The breath is short and quick. Through your nose. So fire away for a minute, stop anytime you felt dizzy.

When you have hit a minute breathe in deeply move the arms together. So that the thumbs are touching. Hold your breath for a count of ten, then breathe out slowly. As you breathe out, bring your arms slowly down to your lap but keep your arms extended until you reach your lap. I recommend doing this for thirty days consistently. See how much calmer and centered you will feel. But getting mostly rid of your ego! Reducing anxiety and those negative thoughts.

Meditation

I highly recommend it. But it isn't for everyone. I have got other techniques you can use to hack your brain to be calmer. I have listed them in another chapter.

This chapter is a tiny flavour of what its benefits are, what it has done for me and some good practises I recommend.

To get you hacking your brain. There is a stat that said people who meditate are healthier and more willing to change themselves and the world.

I get many people telling me that if meditation is so great why isn't it everywhere and done in schools? It is in schools and it is expanding. But there is a fear, a stigma that people feel you have to be a stereotypical description of a hippy. That it's stupid. What effect will it have on me? And some aren't prepared to put in the time and focus or the perseverance to change you. It scares people but what happens if this works? Having more power and control over my life? Over my anxiety? Able to see a life beyond the one I have. One that is amazing? That change can be scary as hell! But ultimately the most rewarding.

This Chapter in a Nutshell

- Studies have proven meditation works. It gives you the space to see your thoughts and react to them.

- They have proven that meditation can have improve your life straight away and can reduce your anxiety by 50 percent in a month. It requires meditation every day and for at least 10 minutes.

- Your biological age is reduced for each year you meditate. By a year! This study took your sight, blood pressure and hearing and compared it to the average of that age group. One study saw that a 60-year-old man had the biological body of a 48-year-old.

- Want to change, to preserve, to understand that life will get in the way. But your determination and need to meditate will be key to whether you become successful with it. If you don't believe, it will help. It won't.

- There are thousands of practises you can use to aid in your anxiety. I would recommend simple ones to start. From just listening to music and feeling it to more advanced forms such as the ego eradicator.

- Want to take your life to another level? Then meditation is key.

BODY

What You Eat!

'I need to do more. I need to make sure that my moods are better by what I eat. I need to manage my anxiety. My diet will get substantially better. I will be substantially better!'

What Is in This Chapter?

How you think and feel depends on what comes from your gut. The vagus nerve directly communicates with the brain and the gut. Your brain and gut are also connected through feelings. There are chemicals called neurotransmitters that live in your brain. So for example, serotonin that controls your happiness and body clock is produced by your gut used for your brain. Also, there are brain chemicals in your immunity system! Your body communicates with you all the time and vice versa.

You need to understand that by helping your anxiety, it matters what your diet is and how you are feeling physically and mentally. If your body feels low, you will feel low. The same can be true of your mind to your body. Many studies have shown those with anxiety and depression have a lower immunity. It really is true that what you are what you eat. I want to give you as many foods that can help you improve your mood, reduce your anxiety and make you feel energized. With being healthier as a bonus.

I want to choose the right foods for you. It should be something you enjoy eating. With the opportunity to choose what ones work best for you. I will give you a list here with their benefits. I will also put this as part of the seven-day action plan.

I want to give you alternatives rather than say don't do something. So, for example, rather than having coffees full of sugar and teas you can have alternatives such as green tea or fruit teas. Which have awesome benefits or dark chocolate, yep that right! It helps with anxiety; it's been scientifically proven!

There are loads of foods that can reduce stress, anxiety and depression. However, I will only pick the ones I feel will help you and the ones I feel that are the best in order to reduce a feeling of overwhelm and having too much information to take in.

What Effect It Will Have on You

One of the biggest consequences I've had with my anxiety is the major damage to my teeth. Too much chocolate, too much sugar and caffeine fuelled coffees. Too much processed foods. Too much sugar everywhere! It has helped me, given me the drive to my day so I can get stuff done, as I fight my anxiety. But it has come at a serious consequence. I hate my teeth now. I am ashamed of them. Although I religiously brush them. I have caused serious irreversible damage to them.

The effect changing your diet will have on you will mean you have more energy. You will feel less exhausted. You will also have more energy the end of the day and won't be damaging your body further like I have with my teeth.

The Mind and Eating

One of the first obstacles you need to overcome and reframe is your mind. I would suggest you record through a journal what you eat during your day. I would recommend that you are honest. It's only you that will see what you have written. You can easily pick up a diary and write. Then you can see patterns to what you eat and when.

When you are about to eat, mindfully meditate. Breathe in deeply but slowly. Ask yourself *What is the reason for eating now?'* Wait for the answer, with no judgements. If you don't get a response, ask again. The answer will fascinate you. This also aids in taking your mind out of the emotional side of the brain and into the more logical side. You can then see if you are eating because you need to or because you want to. Being aware of why is important. Knowledge is power.

The difference to you being successful is how you approach it and what you say to yourself. Come at it with trepidation and worry? Guess what will happen? You will be in a tug of war. One side battling to do and implement what is needed. With another side that won't let you make the changes. You need to make sure you keep calm. I would recommend mediation. Coming at this with a sense of curiosity and fun. Be kind and understanding to yourself and treat yourself like you would your closest, best friend. Be kind and considerate. You are doing your best. If one day it doesn't quite go well. That's fine. There is always tomorrow to get it better. Just don't give up or put things off.

Energy Levels

One of the biggest things for anxiety sufferers is a constant exhaustion. I intend to help you with certain foods to increase your energy levels and give you a better chance of fighting anxiety. What you put in your mouth has a massive difference to how you think and feel.

Remove Sugar

Ok, I'm going to cut to the chase on this. One of the biggest challenges you will have in combating anxiety will be removing sugars or drastically reducing sugars from your diet. I don't mean natural sugars present in bananas, other fruits and vegetables. I am referring to added sugars available in abundance in energy drinks, soft drinks, processed food, flavoured yogurts and condiments you put on your dinner. Like barbecue sauce, salad cream and tomato ketchup as a few examples.

Will this be easy? Hell NO!
Will this be rewarding? Most definitely.

It will reduce your mood swings. It will cut out the energy spikes that keep you going, but it will also remove the huge crashes you have when the sugar runs out. An interesting point to note, it reduces inflammation of the body, I found that surprising.

What Do I Need to Do?

Check the labels on these products and see the levels of sugar. It would amaze you at how high some products are. I would also recommend certain foods to remove or cut back drastically on. To give you the opportunity you really drive yourself.

I have a few things that will help you with your energy kicks. But these are more natural.

I Am on This Journey and This Is What I Am Learning

Since I cut out teas and coffees I have put on weight. I had used sugary foods, like chocolate to stabilise my moods, to make me feel happy, or give me energy spikes.

Removing caffeine has meant I haven't had an anxiety attack/panic attack for around 18 months. But the caffeine would burn through more calories as my body would be full of anxiety. I'd feel the spike of the sugar and then the slump. Boy, would I feel grumpy after the quick burst.

I have found alternative foods to help me which I will list below. There are some, like salmon (yuck). I don't like, but they are excellent food sources to improve your nutrition and lessen anxiety's grip on you.

Water

It can't be agreed how much water the human body needs. Despite many studies and tests. My rule of thumb is when I feel tired, I drink water. The first sign of dehydration or feeling thirsty isn't feeling thirsty. It's feeling tired. Your whole body needs water: 60 percent of your body is water, and ninety percent of your blood is water!

When you get that tired feeling ask yourself when you last drank? I don't mean soda or anything full of sugar. Or teas or coffees. But drank water? If it is ages ago, then drink. It would surprise you how much energy this gives you. And tiredness will be gone.

I still mistake hunger for thirst so will have something to fill me up. Drinking water can be used as part of a weight loss program. I will have water and almonds together. Which also helps to suppress my appetite. Reducing the risk of eating cr*p I don't really need to eat. I go to the toilet a lot more but there are well over fifteen benefits of drinking water.

Some of the best reasons to drink more water:

- It forms mucus and saliva. You need this!

- It lubricates your joints—Fact 80% of the joints around the body are water.

- It helps with weight loss.

- It improves skin health and beauty.

- It delivers oxygen throughout the body. This improves your mood and gives you more energy.

- It regulates your body temperature. Important in helping reduce anxiousness and feeling fed up.

- Helps maintain blood pressure. Keeping you calmer.

Lemons

I have recently learnt a cool hack. One of the last things I do at night is cut half a lemon and put it in a chilled bottle of water. Allowing it to marinate overnight. I usually make two, so I can have one in the morning and one to take to work.

I use this as my energy push. I usually drink two a day. On the way to work and in the middle of the day to keep my energy levels up.

It has been proven having a lemon reduces blood pressure. Something as sufferers know a lot about.

Lemons Have Excellent Qualities but Also a Few Things to Be Wary of

They help your breath smell good, however, it has been known to strip your enamel on your teeth. They have recommended that when you drink you use a straw and wash your mouth out afterwards.

Almonds

I use these often. Bland to taste but give you energy boosts naturally, done over a longer period and helps to reduce your weight. I found this an excellent snack rather than eating the usual s**t I have been in the past. I eat a lot. Not able to stop most of the time.

What Are Almonds Benefits?

- Almonds have several superb benefits. They are:

- Almonds can reduce your blood pressure!

- They are an excellent snack that reduces food intake.

- It also has magnesium, which has been linked in the reduction of anxiety.

- They also contain zinc which help stabilise your mood.

It has been shown that with just a handful of almonds a day you will be 20% less likely to suffer chronic illness, like cancer. If you eat them over a 30-year period compared to those that don't.

Green Tea

This a great opportunity for you to swap out your high caffeine content with a healthier alternative. One that tastes better. I don't recommend too much caffeine since it is a stimulant, but it can carry excellent benefits to you. My thoughts are that green tea has less caffeine in it. So it reduces the risk of higher levels of anxiety. Too much caffeine mimics our fight-or-flight response.

BBC Good Food magazine recommends a higher-priced green tea as some lower-priced products have fluoride in them. They describe green tea as 'The healthiest beverage on the planet!'

Here are a few reasons . . .

1. It reduces inflammation and fights cancer.

2. It aids in reducing the aging process.

3. It improves brain function and makes you smarter.

4. It reduces anxiety!

5. More stable energy than when you drink coffee

6. Increases fat burning and improves your physical performance.

Before I researched this book, I had gone around 18 months with no caffeine. I did like what that it used it to fire my anxiety up. I had spikes of energy. But the comedown made me grumpy, miserable and horrible to be around. My family got me when I was at my worse. I made a decision that caffeine was a drink that the old me had. I never want that person back. There was a fear that if I gave in to it I would slide into him again.

Researching the book has changed my mind completely. The benefits far outweigh my fears.

I highly recommend changing over from higher caffeine content drinks. It can be done over a long period so as not to cut it out straight away.

Chamomile

Calmly influences people. I grow it in my garden. I love smell of it. What I love to do in the summer rub leaves in between my fingers and breathe in. I feel calmer just by smelling it. Many people use it in tea. It has helped many conditions, including sleep disorders and anxiety, because it calms you.

Drinking camomile tea before bed has proven to increase your quality of sleep. A study over a two-week period showed a significant improvement in sleep quality.

I have general anxiety disorder so chamomile directly helps. However, it can help with other forms of anxiety and depression. Its main benefit helps reduce the worrying and restlessness that anxiety brings. Mighty handy when needing to go sleep.

Using chamomile long-term has found no serious side effects. So a win-win all round.

Dark Chocolate

Oh yes! I love this. Chocolate is my biggest downfall. I find that I can cheer myself up by having chocolate. I used it as a mood improver. Makes me feel happy. It has been scientifically proven to improve blood flow to the brain and increase your ability to react to stressful situations.

Chocolate is high in calories. So I would recommend only using dark chocolate in moderation.

I have chocolate that improves my mood. I love chocolate but it hurts because I eat too much of it.

A study showed that to have 40 grams a day for two weeks has shown to reduce anxiety. But please eat it in moderation. Don't be like me.

Yogurts!

This is mainly for probiotic yogurts that has shown great improvement in the health of the brain and brain function. It needs to have live active cultures on the product for this to benefit. We know from a previous chapter that improving the gut has a positive impact on the brain. Yogurts are one of the best.

Some benefits:

- A better functioning brain

- Aids in the control of your mood.

Blueberries

Again you can use blueberries as a replacement for sugary products. Blueberries are a little different from the others listed. It is the one I recommend the most out of all the foods!

When we are full of anxiety and stressed, our bodies need vitamin C which is what blueberries are packed full of. It also helps with oxidative stress. I will be talking about this later in my magic pill chapter. They have shown blueberries not only help reduce anxiety but also help to prevent the causes of anxiety! They have described it as a superfood. I can see why. Of all the foods I recommend in this chapter, this one is probably the most important.

The biggest benefit is that blueberries help to prevent spikes in cortisol, a stress hormone, reducing the feelings of anxiety.

Asparagus

Asparagus can also be an aphrodisiac so be careful with this one!

Anxiety has been linked to low levels of folic acid in the body. Asparagus is packed full of folic acid!

Salmon

I'm not a great lover of salmon. I don't like it at all. However, they have proven it to help with anxiety. Researchers at Ohio State University have found that eating twelve to fifteen ounces of salmon can reduce anxiety by over twenty percent! The fatty Acids in a salmon can calm your mood.

Putting This All Together

I have given you a selection. You can put this all together in the 7-day plan at the end of the book. I will give you a structure to aid you.

There are many more superfoods you can use to aid in your sleep, your mood or your anxiety. Feeling better about yourself is an important step. Feeling happier and healthier will give you an excellent foundation to take on your anxiety. To feel you are at your peak physically and mentally will give you the belief, momentum and faith you WILL break this.

How Will You Feel?

There are several other excellent foods and supplements I will go into detail later in the book. To give you even more heart, strength and hope you can smash this. But knowing eating healthier, feeling happier, feeling empowered and being at your best will give you all the leverage you need to do this.

ONE ASK!

Don't just read this chapter, or the book and not do anything. Make a change NOW. Today is your first day of change. Kick the old habits of eating processed food, coffees, teas and energy drinks (URGH!) to the curb. We still haven't had enough clinical studies on what energy drinks do to your mind and body. I know what it did when I drank them: super focussed, anxiety right up and driven. But the comedown was horrible: exhausted, irritable, stomach pains and depressed. It would literally take me days to recover from taking one. Let alone the amount people take these days. My opinion of energy drinks are they are one of the worse things you can have for anxiety and depression. It's the exact opposite of what you should drink!

The old standards of wallowing in your own self pity and not doing anything are over. You have the power now. YOU KNOW what you need to do. Scared? Good, be scared. It means that this will make a difference and you can do this. Question is: Dare you try?

This Chapter in a Nutshell

- Adding certain foods to your diet like dark chocolate, salmon, avocados and lemons can increase your energy, mood and aid your anxiety.

- An obvious comment, but one that needs repeating: cut back on processed foods, coffee, tea and alcohol. You will see a large spike in energy, but also you will feel more consistent and have less worry about managing your mood swings when the sugary foods wear off.

- This chapter is about giving you a selection of the foods that can improve your physical and mental well being. We will go in more detail later and I will structure it in the 7-day action plan at the back of this book.

- You will be empowered. Your emotions will be more consistent. No massive dips or feeling exhausted. It's about taking control of you.

- I do not recommend energy drinks. The cost of taking them means you feel exhausted and full of anxiety. Not worth the risk ever.

- No longer accept your old standard. You need to dare to push yourself further. This

- will make a difference to you and your anxiety. But it needs to be a consistent and conscious effort.

THE MAGIC PILL!

Protandim – LifeVantage

'It's not the miracle drug.
But it's close to it as it can be'
—Gary Stern (Elite distributor at LifeVantage)

What Is in This Chapter?

It explains what the benefits are from clinical trials and it explains what the pills are.

It will go through more of the science behind the drug to give you a clear understanding of the science.

I will go through how it has affected me and improved my life and show you the potential for what it could do for you!

What Are the Benefits?

It will give you a clear understanding of the benefits of using Protandim. Two natural pills called NRF1 and NRF2 that will enhance your life. From better sleep to more energy and focus. Being focused, a good sleep, having energy and feeling happy is the foundation of hacking your brain and body to beat anxiety.

The Science Bit – What Is Protandim and What Does This Mean for Me?

Protandim is a patented product developed by LifeVantage. I am an affiliate of LifeVantage.

The overview is that Protandim produces a three hundred percent increase in glutathione. A key in antioxidants and anti-aging. As your health decreases as you get older the likelihood of serious illnesses and diseases increases. These can include cancer, diabetes, etc.

But this isn't all. I will go into more detail later, but LifeVantage has produced two little pills one that aids in and produces better sleep, a key step to smashing your anxiety. And another pill you can use to increase your energy levels, that has the ingredients to improve your oxidative stress—ageing: Oxidative stress is just a fancy term for the ageing process.

They had it under supplements but this is because they don't have a section that will do it justice yet! Because the science is above ANYTHING on the market.

In clinical trials done outside LifeVantage it has been discovered that taking Protandim can increase your oxidative stress (this is found in blueberries but you will need to eat thousands to get near to this pill) by up to forty percent in thirty days and seventy percent in ninety . . .

I have a lady that will explain later in this book about the effect taking it has had on her. But there are many studies that support this pill. I invite you to Google it. Do your own research. Discover yourself what this pill can do.

NRF1 – What the Hell Is That?

The short of it is that it activates parts of your brain that encourage a better night's sleep. This is the key thing with both pills. They don't give you anything extra that is not in the body. Rather it activates parts of your body giving YOU a better, more efficient night's sleep.

What Are the Benefits of Using It?

Mitochondria are the workhorses of our cells. Mitochondria is where the cell gets its energy from and powers the rest of the cell and uses 95 percent of the energy that your body produces. Over time, as the body gets older they get less efficient and produce less. So you have less energy. This is where NRF1 comes in. It activates more mitochondria and protects the ones you have.

What NRF1 Does:

- Increases cellular energy.

- Improves cellular performance.

- Enhances cellular health.

- Promotes cellular repair.

- Improves sleep quality.

- Boosts Mitochondria production.

- Boosts the ability to network.

- Slows cellular aging down.

This means that your cells function at their peak performance. This isn't about taking a pill to improve your health. This is activating your body to do it for you. Using natural products!

Taking the crazy yellow pill can make the difference to those that have struggled with alcoholism, ADHD, panic attacks, manic depression, schizophrenia to name a few examples. It could make the difference if they are showing the signs/symptoms of what I described above. This is just a tiny selection. I will repeat this again. There are over 200 different illnesses related to oxidative stress. I have read and seen testimonies from some of these 'conditions'. There have been massive improvements.

I know several people that have said their anxiety has been massively improved because they are taking Protandim. Panic/anxiety attacks are a thing of the past because they have used it.

NRF1 helps you have a far better sleep which aids in you feeling better about yourself and emotionally better to take on the day.

NRF2 helps you have more energy and reduces inflammation. All those aches and pains you have will be less.

Don't expect to feel massively different. There are subtle changes. Our brains have an annoying habit of resetting ourselves as we are constantly changing. So we don't see the improvements in ourselves. This where journaling comes in.

What I Have Felt

I can do more these days. I am able to do far more work, like the physical labour of my job, and still have energy left over. This has come in part by my mediation, but also due to taking the pills.

I have felt that I don't ache so much after a hard day at work. The same thing can be said for that night and for the next few days afterwards.

The biggest thing I have felt is more focussed and completely driven on one purpose. It has come with my willingness to push myself and have clear goals. Many people I have spoken to have commented on how much more driven I am now. I was driven before, but now it has gone up several levels.

I can sleep a lot better. I now find that it is very rarely that I don't get the full eight hours I need to be mentally ready, focused and well every day. To be my best me I can be.

On the rare occasion I don't sleep (this is very rare, three times in five months), I still feel considerably better than if I didn't take it.

Why I Recommend It over Antidepressants

Firstly, a disclaimer: I am NOT a medical professional. It is important to seek medical advice when contemplating medications and supplements. However, from my experience with many people and the extensive reading I have done on the subject, I feel there needs to be another way of helping people with anxiety and depression. Antidepressants aren't it. They treat the symptoms, not the cause. The body gets used to that level and then you have to increase the dosage to feel okay again. People don't look at fixing their anxiety or depression when they are feeling okay. But that is what I highly recommend. So that when you stop the dam doesn't come crashing around you. That you feel ten times worse than you did before you went on it.

The biggest worry for me is some side effects. I won't bore you with all of them. But the biggest one is suicidal thoughts! That's right, you can have suicidal thoughts when taking medication! The worst thing you should feel when you are on antidepressants. I know that people on medication are constantly monitored, but this is a scary thought.

I have said this previous, but it's worth repeating. The percentage of how much it helps in studies is 30 percent. I know many people say it's helped them, and that's great. But that is the same level as if someone gives you a placebo, and saying it will help and the person believing it.

I go in to detail in this book about energy levels, but having Protandim gives you higher energy levels, reduces inflammation and aids your sleep. Coupled with a huge reduction in oxidative stress. The only people they don't recommend taking Protandim are those people who have had a transplant in their past. Taking this pill will give you a springboard to a better future and its natural with no serious side effects. Would that interest you?

What Is Important to Note

For the levels to go up to the required amount it takes time for the pills to work. This depends on how old you are, to how long that takes. This allows the activation to get the body back to the required level. This takes time. Three hundred percent is amazing, but that too requires time to do its thing.

So for the body to get to the level you would need it to be for a twenty-year-old you would need two months; a thirty-year-old three months; forty-year-old, four months; fifty-year-old, five months. And so on.

So, for example, it will take me one month for each decade.

If you are still curious and what to find out more, then I recommend googling it and researching yourself. There is a whole host of trials that have proven that it works!

The Long-Term Benefits!

Testimonials from people that have lost weight, feel healthier, look healthier and done amazing things.

Since I have been taking it, I have gone from writing a book in eleven months to getting this book done in just seven weeks. My focus has completely changed.

Some people have said their arthritis has gone in six months. Others that have seen great improvements in their son's ADHD to people showing improvements after fighting cancer.

This Chapter in a Nutshell

- I am an affiliate of Protandim a natural 'supplement'

- Through many clinical trials it has been proven to reduce oxidative stress (cellular aging) by up to 40 percent in 30 days and 70 in 90 days.

- There are two different pills NRF1 and NRF2. One aids in a better, far stronger sleep and the other gives you energy and reduces inflammation. Put together they are stronger.

- They are natural ingredients that activate your mitochondria.

- They can increase your mitochondria levels by 300 percent!

- There are over 200 illnesses, diseases, etc. That are caused by oxidative stress. This is about prevention. By taking them it significantly lowers the risk of receiving these diseases.

- I have seen and spoken to people that have seen dramatic improvements in many mental health struggles. Many have reported improvements in themselves. One lady since taking it hasn't had a panic attack (I have a testimony—chat about this in a later chapter)

- Since taking them, I have a better sleep, have more energy and have become even more determined and driven.

- I think antidepressants aren't working like they should and this is an excellent alternative to them. I would always recommend speaking to a medical professional before changing or deciding about stopping or changing your pills.

- Being able to sleep better and higher energy levels is a great springboard to take on your anxiety.

- Mitochondria is the workhorse of your cells.

Anxiety Testimony

PJ is an amazing woman. Recently she announced that she has gone over year since a panic attack! She cites Life-Vantage as a major player in her life change.

She has become an inspiration to so many people. It delighted me that she wanted to help me with this book. This is her story.

How Long Have You Struggled with Anxiety?

I can remember having anxiety young, but it wasn't until I got older that it became a problem.

When I had my first pregnancy, my gynecologist started asking questions about mood and thoughts. My husband, who I've been married to for 10 years now also pointed out some of my behaviours that he thought were a bit over the top. Such as expecting way too much of myself, trying to have too much control, anxious around people, etc.

How Did You Feel When You Were at Your Worst before Taking Protandim?

I've had several occasions where my panic has frightened my children, I'm not proud of that and it motivates me to do whatever it takes to stay strong.

Just unshakable fear and nervousness all the time. Thinking strangers are going to hurt me or take my children. Unable to relax and just enjoy the moment. Deciding that I'm better at home, in my safe space with no interruptions. That's where I maintain control . . . when I step out my front door I lose that control.

When Did You First Take Protandim?

I ran from Protandim for a year because I saw it as false hope. After a day with multiple panic attacks I decided to try it.

How Has It Helped You?

After about two weeks I noticed a change in my breathing and the tightness in my chest was reducing. I remember coming home and telling my husband, "I took a deep breath today." He was confused . . . lol It felt heavenly . . . to fill my lungs with air. Something about it was causing me to relax more. There was no anxiety over taking it because I know it's plants, so I stuck with it. I haven't missed a day in a year.

Aside from the breathing, I noticed I was falling asleep better and getting up easier. I lost the craving for Diet Coke so I wasn't drinking it every day. I started to feel like I had control over what I wanted to get done in a day and what I didn't.

Some days the anxiety is there, but I can tell that my body is responding to it and fighting back. A couple times I have felt a panic attack coming, but it never reaches the surface. It subsides.

What Advice Would You Give to Someone That Is Curious about Protandim?

Do some research, the science is there. There are thousands of testimonies out there. Don't expect it to work overnight because it's natural. It takes your body time to do what it needs to do.

What Has the Biggest Benefit Been Taking It?

It has led me to research more all natural methods to caring for my body without harmful drugs that have side effects. I've learned so much about why my body responds to life the way it does. I'm holding MYSELF accountable for the choices I make and instead of saying, "There is something wrong with me." I'll say, "What have I eaten? How much sleep did I get last night? What is my body trying to tell me? What are my thoughts?"

Anything Else You Would Like to Say?

I don't know how this demon called "Anxiety" made its way into my life, but it is not welcome and I'm not going to just lay down and let him stay. I will fight for my husband, my children, and my family. I urge people to never say, "MY" Anxiety . . . to me that is owning it, and it's not yours, never was meant to be a part of you. We are called to be and do so much more.

If you would like to know more about PJ Addairs journey or you would like to know more about her please visit https://b-m.facebook.com/eatpraytrain1/

7-DAY ACTION PLAN

Undo – Start – Continue

A simple but easy-to-use, follow and digest plan to supercharge you!

You can pick what you like.

If you don't like it or it tastes bad, that's fine. Stop.

If it isn't working for you. That's fine to stop.

This is here to help you. So you can pick what's best for you!

Don't think you HAVE to do all. Try some. If they don't work, that's fine. Intuitively choose them to come up with the best for your structure.

Choose one thing from each section—start, stop and undo.

Monday Getting a Structure

Day one of your new better you. This is about choosing what will help you structure your day. So they become rituals you do without thinking. Pick three from this list.

Start

- Before you get up out of bed mediate.

- Make your first cup of tea/coffee in the morning a ritual.

- Let the shower clear your stress.

- Box breathing before you get to work.

- Journal down your feelings.

- Mediate at break.

- Take the dog for a walk.

- Go out with nature.

- Any time you get during the day focus on your breath for thirty seconds.

Undo

- Tea and coffee, half your intake.

- Going to go straight for the juggler on this. Cut back to start on your reliance of caffeine to get you through the day.

- If it isn't coffee then energy drinks. The link hasn't been made yet, but I have seen in others and myself. It aids in anxiety, especially, and depression. No matter how good you feel taking them, and most of them are nice to drink, there is a crash point where your anxiety and depression are maxed. With zero energy levels.

Continue

- Take your NRF2 tablet.

- Make Lemon water—make two. I would recommend overnight. Let the lemon mix in with the water.

- If you like dark chocolate, have a piece stashed for today. When you are feeling down.

- Salmon. Put that in your sandwiches.

- Almonds again as an energy boost.

- Bananas reduce anxiety and increase energy levels.

Today is your start.

Keep going with your motivation and enthusiasm. You will find that there will be challenges. It's your belief and willingness to keep going. That is going to be the difference. Structure of your day is meditation three times a day or use OmHarmonics/Bliss.

A few things to consider. Your first few days are going to be challenging. With less caffeine and sugar to boost your energy levels, you may start to worry why you aren't pushing yourself. It will take you a few days to overcome these obstacles. However, taking lemon water and almonds will still give you a better boost.

Calm—Tuesday

Today is managing your moods and anxiety. By putting YOU in the driver's seat. Using some tools that will switch your moods. You find that some will be repeated in other days.

Pick One of the following.

Start

- Enjoy eating your food. Slow up. Can be a great break from anxiety.

- Put your most favourite music on that makes you feel happy and sing along for ten minutes.

- Listen to OmHarmonics with headphones on. Either find some quiet place or whilst doing jobs around the house.

- Notice your thoughts.

- Meditate three times a day.

- Box breathing.

- Notice your breathing three times during the day.

Undo

- Look at better, healthier foods to eat. Cut back on the processed foods and ready meals. If it means you need make the dinner the night before, do so. This is about supercharging you up. Helping you to feel sharper, more energetic and full of fight!

- Victim mode not willing to drive yourself forward. Understanding that this is a slow battle and not giving up at the first hurdle. Draw a line. This is the line I REFUSE to go behind.

- Getting calm requires you to protect yourself from anxiety. Being calm when your anxiety kicks off is a far stronger place to be than not. That's what you need to get yourself to.

Continue

- Building your structure. Getting the right foods in. Taking your Protandim NRF1 twenty minutes before bed and NRF2 with your breakfast.

- Experimenting with different ways to get calm. Find the best ones that work for you.

Exercise & Sleep—Wednesday

Getting your body moving even to take a walk in nature will have an improvement on your sleep. Choose from the following. Make sure you give yourself the best opportunity to sleep at night.

Start—Choose from One of the Following

- Go out in nature. Enjoy the woods or forest.

- Make sleep—going to sleep at a regular time a routine.

- Make exercise part of your daily ritual. Take a walk.

- Make sure you have ten minutes of you time. Alone to your thoughts. Every day.

- Take a brisk walk in the afternoon, take your dog and slow down your world for ten minutes.

- Take a walk in the morning before you start your day.

Undo

- Replace caffeine and high sugar drinks with a healthy start to your day packed full of energy.

- Replace ten minutes watching television going out.

- Don't drink alcohol after 8pm at night. Make sure you have no or little alcohol in your bloodstream before going to bed to avoid a disruptive sleep.

- No caffeine after 4pm. Replace it with green tea, such as chamomile, instead.

- Know of the stories you tell yourself for not exercising or being active enough.

- Rather than drive for a short journey, walk. Save on petrol and improves your mood.

Continue

- Drinking lemon water when you are feeling tired. It's a sign you are thirsty! It will give yourself an energy kick.

- Slowing yourself down. Especially your rapid mind.

- Challenge your thoughts. Ask yourself what does this mean?

- Keep a journal.

Thursday—Anxiety Reduction

Mixing in the right foods is integral to aid the management of your anxiety. The choices given below are to ensure that you have the power to reduce your anxiety at will.

Start

- Box breathing.

- Meditate.

- Understand your own anxiety triggers.

- Slow yourself down.

- Eating salmon, probiotic yogurts and almonds.

Undo

- Stop being so hard on yourself.

- Do not skip meals!

- Don't ignore anxiety inducing problems in your life take them head on!

- Fix a consistent repetitive stress.

- Focus on making your daily routines consistent and rituals you do every day out of habit.

Continue

- Believe in yourself—you have got this!

- Celebrate every success even if its small.

- Setting yourself challenging but achievable goals every day.

- Review and reflect on how you are getting on.

Happy—Friday

Get your bliss! Understand that you can feel whatever you want to.

Start

- Find something you love to do and do it for at least thirty minutes a day. It could be something like painting, drawing, reading or writing.

- Practice smiling in the mirror.

- Look in the mirror and find an inspiring quote that makes you feel happy. Recite it. But really feel it. Watch yourself when you are doing it.

- Set up a bliss board 'All the Things You Are Happy About' in your life!

Undo

- Get out of bed. The alarm goes get up. Break that habit.

- Learn to let go of things that are worrying you.

- Appreciate the world you have.

- Stop expecting you will be happy when X happens.

- Allowing your negative emotions to control you.

- Allowing yourself to be constantly sad.

Continue

- To be kind to yourself. You will make mistakes. You will get things wrong. Understand that it will take you time.

- Each day is a new day.

- Get clear on what you want out of life, live and be the person you want to be NOW.

- Set yourself boundaries.

- Understand that we create our own world by what we feel and do.

- Be careful what questions you ask yourself.

- Be yourself.

Saturday—What Is Your Anxiety?

Learn the triggers of what sets you off!

Start

- Write done from 1 to 10 what your biggest fears are. Write your own list of your own worries. Keep this list as this is an important part of your battle.

- Write a journal and see what your thoughts are telling you. Note and review them.

- Start with the intention that today you will beat this, one day at a time.

Undo

- Swap out high caffeinated drinks for green tea. We have discussed the benefits of this drink. Find one that you love drinking. It may seem expensive but same price as a coffee at Starbucks.

- You are what you eat. Cut back on the food that up your anxiety.

- Drinking only 3 cups of caffeine a day. One can be green tea. The other of your choice.

Continue

- Anxiety takes time.

- Understand that anxiety will do all it can to keep you safe. Safe in your little box.

- Find people that will support, guide and help you. Find people where you belong.

- Slow down your mind. Your day should be about slowing down your thoughts. So you can think.

- Giving yourself kindness and compassion.

Your Beliefs—Sunday

What you tell yourself is what you believe you are!

Start

- Making smoothies for your breakfast. All about giving you energy for the morning.

- Listening to YouTube clips for inspiration.

- Google and find inspiring words that will keep you motivated.

- Recording experiences that have made you feel happy. So you can use them in future when you are feeling down.

- Look for people with a similar outlook that will inspire you to push on.

- Find role models that you admire and that you can learn from.

Continue

- You now have a daily plan. Stick to it. If you need to go back and follow it again, I highly recommend you do so!

- Challenge your stories and beliefs.

- Use the questions from your beliefs written earlier to improve you.

Undo

- Holding onto beliefs that no longer serve you.

- Allowing negative beliefs to sap your self-confidence.

- Allowing your old habits to define you now.

- Allowing negative feelings to drag you down.

- Allow negative people to drag you down.

Ten Questions

Rate these questions using:
<u>Never</u>, <u>sometimes</u>, <u>often</u>, <u>all the time</u>

How often do you feel happy?

How calm do you feel?

How often do you get a good night's sleep?

How easily do you decide?

How often do you feel nervous?

How often do you feel irritable and restless?

How often do you feel tired?

How often do you feel sad?

How often do you feel useless?

How often do you struggle to calm down when something upsets you?

Additional questions—These just need to be recorded.

How many cups of high caffeine do you drink a day?

How often a day do you meditate?

Or practice getting calm?

Your Beliefs

This is for you to record and review again after you have implemented this book and reviewed. Please be as honest as possible. This is to see your beliefs. Where you are at right now. NO judgements. Only YOU will see this.

You can answer these statements with a true or false. What you feel.

I feel like a victim. Everything is my fault.

What is wrong with me?

I don't deserve the best life possible.

I can't handle failure.

Rejection I can handle.

I can't take criticism.

If I work at it, I can have What I want.

I am good enough.

Life is too hard.

Compare this to you the first one. How much has it changed?

Write your thoughts here . . .

What Can You Improve?

Write down here . . .

And So It Ends . . .

'I continue to grow, I continue to have joy in my life, I appreciate the person I am and I am excited for what MY future holds. I now have tools that will help me through all my struggles. I have supplements I now take that have made me feel the most alive I have EVER felt. I feel so optimistic for my future and my anxiety is broken!'

We're at the end. Congratulations. I am delighted you have reached here.

I have enjoyed writing this book. Up to this point, it has been my favourite book to write as it's pushed me beyond my knowledge and beyond my comfort zone.

This book has been far more collaboration gaining knowledge from other people and implementing it in to my rituals than any other books previous.

To learn so much and so many amazing people has been humbling. I love my job of being an author as I get to meet amazing people.

From that there are so many people I need to thank. But I will leave that in the acknowledgements.

I have a testimony from an amazing woman describing her struggle and where she now is in her life. It should encourage you to see what is possible in your world's. What you can do with your life.

I am just an average Joe, look what I've achieved! Look at what more you can achieve. If you continue to implementing this book.

The 7-day action plan is a great way to start off. Use it intuitively. If you don't feel comfortable or doesn't work for you, then stop. You can use this book to help you and use what you need. You can pick what you want, you can customize this book to work for you. You have no excuse for not achieving what you want. The only person who won't achieve is you.

You should now feel amazeballs. Having energy to burn, feeling inspired from the stories I have shared.

I have given you so many hacks to improve your mood and help you feel calmer. In so many and fun places.

You understand you have to be a gatekeeper, but what goes into your mind and what goes into your body. You understand now the link between the body and the mind. They both need to be looked after. Look after your thoughts. Look after you. Your thoughts shape your world. So be very careful what questions you ask your brain. Because it will answer. And most of the time you won't like it!

You must also feel amazing like you were in your twenties. Free of the brain fog in the morning. Free of the aches and pains. That's the power of Protandim. Many athletes are using this now. As a natural remedy.

You have some excellent tools to help you feel calmer. You are eating more healthy. You understand all the problems that can arise from anxiety, but that's okay. Because you have got it covered!

Compare your start score to the end. Has it improved? What else do you need to improve?

You can see that progress! You can see that you are getting better! You should see sizeable jumps in your progress. Giving you the evidence and courage to continue to grow the person you are becoming.

Taking control of your life is an amazing empowering feeling. Doing things that make your body healthier and better is also amazing. You feel inspired to go beyond what you felt is possible. You should feel that you can take on the world now. Doing things on your terms! Not at the mercy of your thoughts, feelings and anxiety.

I made this book like my other books free of most of the jargon. This isn't about overloading you with steps, jobs and things to do. It's a simple and easy-to-implement book. To show you what you can achieve in your world. Your life now is set up to be the person you always wanted to be. A supercharged you!

Are you excited what's next?

I will finish on a quote from an amazing book by Deepak Chopra called *Quantum Healing*

This is my agenda. My goals for you. This is how I feel you what you should believe.

'Your personal agenda

'1. You relax and relinquish the desire to control.

2. You trust that you are cherished in creation, and you act on this trust.

3. You accept your own being as a source of infinite intelligence.

4. You approach every problem as level of solution that can be found.

5. You focus on personal growth, which is external, and minimise personal setbacks, which are temporary.

6. You ask for and receive support from nature.

7. You resist the endless demands and unceasing insecurity of the ego.'

Your world is yours. Get the best from it. *Hack* away!

Want a Free Copy
of My First Book
HOPE OVER ANXIETY?

Please visit:

https://mailchi.mp/f3b44101979d/freeanxietybook

Did You Enjoy
Power over Anxiety?

Would love you to write a review. I know you are really busy. But I would appreciate a few minutes of your time. You only need to put a few lines. That's all it needs.

Are You Curious to Know More about Biohacking?

Would you like to know more about the crazy yellow pill?

Then click the link HERE
www.christophermosswriter.com

Or Email me at mosschristopher799@gmail.com

Bibliography

INTRODUCTION TO BIOHACKING – AR MEISEL

THE HEALING SELF – DEEPAK CHOPRA

QUANTUM HEALING – DEEPAK CHOPRA

Acknowledgments

I am so privileged to continue to meet so many amazing people in my life. I have learned a great deal from so many of them.

To Jessica Perez her drive, willingness to help, not to gain anything, but just help has been a humbling and inspiring experience.

Gary Stern, Boyd Barlow and so many other great people from LifeVantage.

To Kelly Walker Hines, who continues to be a great champion to the cause.

To PJ Addair, thank you so much for taking the time to share your story with so many others. Being so open and honest in the process.

To Jill Rodgers it's been awesome to walk the same path with you!

To Deanna Baxter. You have been an amazing support in the last year. Thank you for poring over my manuscript and ripping it to pieces. Then helping polish it into a beautiful book! I have been delighted with working with her over the last year. I wouldn't have achieved what I have this year (publishing 3 books in 4 months) without her support, care and hard work.

Made in the USA
Coppell, TX
09 December 2019

12628879R00116